CW00411568

EERO MÄKELÄ   GERO HOTTINGER   PEKKA IMMONEN

NEW FLAVOURS
FROM FINLAND

PHOTOGRAPHS BY KAJ G. LINDHOLM

Otava Publishing Co. Ltd. Helsinki

Editor: PEKKA RÅMAN
English translation: HILDI HAWKINS
Graphic design: KATJA ALANEN

Printed in Finland by Otava Printing Works
Keuruu 1995

ISBN 951-1-13811-1

WELCOME

TO THE

FINNISH TABLE

F ood and music recall one another in many respects. They are the most international areas of culture, because to experience them does not demand words or translations.

Little wonder, then, that the world of taste is our common property. It is difficult to imagine a national food culture in which we would not find influences borrowed from our neighbours' tables. And it would surely be equally difficult to find a gastronomic culture lacking its own, quite unique, special characteristics. We have sometimes pondered why national food traditions have, in recent times, become some of the most important inspirations of gastronomy — and not just in Finland, but almost everywhere in the world.

The answer no doubt lies, here as in so many other matters, in internationalisation.

The rapid communication of knowledge and experiences and the uniformity of customs and eating habits that follows drives creative people — chefs among them — to seek new, fresh interpretations of familiar old themes. And a knowledge of one's own culture is, after all, a definite advantage in understanding other cultures.

New Flavours from Finland is, definitively, a Finnish recipe book. Through it, we invite you to journey to the roots of Finnish gastronomic culture, to a country where four seasons, and East and West, meet.

But in addition to the unique history of Finnish gastronomic culture, we should like to introduce you to the unique, international future of our gastronomy.

We hope this journey will leave a good taste in your mouth.

SPRING

DAY

IS LONGER

THAN NIGHT

ONCE MORE

For winterweary Finns, the spring equinox, 21 March, means the end of the long, dark winter, although visitors may feel that the winter is then at its best. The snow is still firm enough for skiing and the ice of the lakes for ice-fishing, but the Finns can already smell the scent of the coming spring and wait impatiently for the first snowdrops and crocuses to blossom in their gardens.

Easter Sunday falls on the Sunday following the first full moon after the spring equinox. In Finland, the celebration of this, the oldest church festival, shows the clear influence of the Orthodox church and the culture of the east.

For the 60,000-odd members of the Russian Orthodox church, Easter means both a joyful festival and the end of the longest fast of the year. And after the fast,

the delicacies of the heavily laden feast tables of the Orthodox tradition have found their way on to the Easter tables of other Finns.

A joint of lamb or young mutton is the main course of the Easter table.

It was put into the great baking ovens of former times in a wooden trough or *särä* as much as a metre and a half long. At first only the meat was put in the *särä*, but from the 19th century onward this was accompanied by chopped vegetables, such as swede, turnip and carrot.

Because eggs, milk and cream were among the foods forbidden during the Lenten fast, it was natural for them to be used all the more generously in traditional Easter dishes, and particulary in desserts.

This celebration of rebirth also marked the end of winter, and the beginning of the difficult period before the new season's new growth could be harvested – so a little luxury was in order.

A cake of curd cheese made in the form of a truncated pyramid, *pasha*, and the sweet *baba* and *kulits* pastries, are typical Orthodox Easter desserts, whose preparation has spread throughout the country from eastern Finland.

Pasha is a centuries-old Easter dish whose preparation in the authentic manner demanded time and patience. Before the industrial preparation of curd cheese, the necessary curds were made by heating soured milk.

Made of curd cheese, egg-yolks, butter and soured cream, the delicious *pasha* can be flavoured with your choice of mixed peel, raisins, almonds, vanilla or nuts, and it is then strained through a wooden mould.

The mould is customarily decorated with many different engraved patterns, but all include the letters XB – Christ is risen.

PAINTED EGGS AND
STRANGE-LOOKING *mämmi*

The colouring of eggs is also part of the Orthodox Easter tradition.

Originally, eggs were always coloured red, using onion skins, coffee grounds or rose pigment. As the custom spread, it became a favourite among children. Onion skins were replaced by watercolours, and the 'works of art' themselves acquired a new range of cheerful pigments.

Chocolate eggs later replaced decorated hens' eggs. The first chocolate eggs, mignon eggs, were real eggshells filled with fine chocolate. When the Helsinki confectioner Karl Fazer began to  make them in 1896, the eggshells were filled by hand using a diamond drill.

The strange-looking *mämmi*, too, is a centuries-old Easter dessert. This thick porage, made from sweetened malt and rye flour and stewed for a long time in the oven, originates from south-western Finland, and tastes a great deal better than its appearance might at first lead one to believe.

The Easter tradition also includes witches who, complete with cats and coffee-pots, fly about on their broomsticks on Easter night, and who are known to collect all extraneous wool and scraps of leather.

Witches left Finnish air-space some time ago, but the tradition is continued by little girls dressed up as witches who, on Palm Sunday, go from door to door waving willow-branches decorated with feathers, wishing householders happiness and success and, as a reward, collecting all the sweets that can be found in the house.

WINTER-WANDERED SALMON
AND THE FIRST MORELS OF SPRING

The Finnish morel (*Gyromitra esculenta*), which is similar in appearance to the morels (*Morchella*) which are so popular in Europe, is a spring delicacy much loved by the Finns. Elsewhere it is becoming a rarity: on account of its poisonousness, sale of this wrinkled, dark brown mushroom has been restricted in recent years in many countries.

To remove the poison, morels are blanched carefully in at least two changes of water or dried carefully (and then blanched at least twice before use).

Morels stewed in cream are, in the opinion of many, at their best with spring salmon or whitefish and the first new potatoes of the season.

In the river Teno, which flows along Finland's northernmost border into the Arctic Sea, lives the king of Finnish salmon. Because of its magnificent red flesh and the colour of its covering of scales, it is more distinguished even than its relatives that live in the other famous salmon rivers of Lapland.

Salmon has always had an important place in Finnish food culture. The salmon taken in the Gulf of Finland and the Gulf of Bothnia have been plentiful from decade to decade. To the extent that, even a hundred years ago, it was customary for servants' contracts on the salmon rivers of northern Ostrobothnia to specify that salmon was not to be given to serving staff more than six times a week!

Which is better, sea whitefish or lake whitefish? Each has its supporters, but they are united in the opinion that whitefish is at its most flavourful in spring and early summer – and that the best way to serve it is *gravad*, or lightly salted. Real gastronomists claim that *gravad* whitefish is finer in flavour even than *gravad lax*.

Whitefish is also excellent fried as fillets, or baked whole in the oven. Grilled on an open fire, or smoked, it forms the climax of many a summer sauna night.

W hat could be a better accompaniment to salmon than the spring's first, freshly picked spinach? Finns used also to remedy their after-winter iron deficiency by eating slightly more unusual early plants.

For example, the young, delicate green nettle is a mild and excellent source of iron. Nettles are made into stews and soups, like spinach. They are also used to flavour bread.

Spring rhubarb makes a delicious pie or fruit soup, which was once among the most popular Finnish home-cooked desserts.

THE FIRST OF MAY IS
OFFICIALLY THE FIRST DAY OF SPRING,
EVEN IF IT RAINS CATS AND DOGS

Many Finns still remember one beautiful, hot Mayday – the oldest may even remember two. Everyone, on the other hand, remembers

a freezing cold, rainy or snowy Mayday. Nevertheless, Mayday is the spring festival, the greatest (and only) carnival of the year. A bigger carnival is known to have been celebrated on only one occasion, when Finland won its first ice hockey world championship in May 1995.

The celebration of Mayday begins on the previous evening, when the streets and restaurants of the city are filled to bursting with carnival folk and white-hatted students waving balloons and Mayday whisks.

Sima, or mead, is drunk on Mayday, the drink of the ancient Vikings, which is fermented from water, brown sugar, yeast, honey and lemon juice. Mayday cookies (*tippaleipä*) – deep-fried pastries – are eaten with *sima*.

Because it has become the custom to enjoy, along with mild home-brewed *sima*, plentiful amounts of industrially produced Finnish and foreign sparkling wines, it is highly understandable that the various pickled fish and ice-cold *schnapps* on offer at Mayday lunches are most welcome. The first of May is probably the only day when almost all the restaurants are full to the last seat. If you want to take part, remember to reserve your table in good time!

4–5 WHITE HERRING FILLETS

1/2 L WHIPPED CREAM

1 DL DRY WHITE WINE

1/2 DL VODKA

1/2 DL SUGAR

2 TBSP CHOPPED DILL OR CHIVES

FINELY GROUND WHITE PEPPER

PARFAIT OF HERRING

■ Dice the herring fillets into cubes the size of the tip of your little finger. Combine all ingredients and pour the mixture into a bread-tin. Place in the freezer for 24 hours.

■ Serve with boiled potatoes and sour-dough rye bread.

Beer or mineral water and a frosted glass of vodka crown this unusual gastronomic experience.

UPSIDE-DOWN VENDACE TART

■ This dish can also be prepared with gudgeons or fresh sardines.

Rinse the vendace quickly in cold water, rinse and dry well. Melt half the butter in a shallow pan and add the bacon and leeks. Simmer for approximately three minutes until soft (do not brown), remove from heat and allow to cool.

Roll out the puff pastry to a thickness of a couple of millimetres, to a circle a little larger than the mould. Grease the base of the mould with the rest of the butter (use it all); season the vendace with salt and a little black pepper. Place the vendace in the mould radially, their tails toward the centre. Make a second layer if necessary. Spread the leek-bacon mixture evenly over the vendace, cover with pastry and push the edge of the pastry between the mould and the fish. Bake in a 180-degree oven for 45 minutes.

■ After removing the tart from the oven, allow it to rest for about five minutes. Then turn the tart out on to a serving plate and serve immediately.

To accompany the dish, you could try the traditional cold buttermilk. Slightly more conventional alternatives are mineral water or a fresh, fruity white wine such as the Austrian Grüner Veltliner.

6—8 SERVINGS

800 G CLEANED VENDACE
100 G BUTTER
100 G BACON, FINELY SLICED
150 G LEEKS, FINELY CHOPPED
300 G PUFF PASTRY
SALT AND ROUGHLY GROUND BLACK PEPPER

SMOKED LAMB AND CABBAGE SOUP

500 G SHOULDER OF LAMB, BONED

2 1/2 L WATER

1 TSP COARSE SALT

300 G STOCK VEGETABLES

3 BAY LEAVES

1/2 TSP WHOLE BLACK PEPPERS

1/2 TSP WHOLE WHITE PEPPERS

500 G WHITE CABBAGE, CHOPPED

100 G CARROTS, CHOPPED

150 G POTATOES, PEELED AND DICED

200 G SMOKED LAMB, BONED

2 TBSP PARSLEY, CHOPPED

■ Fill a saucepan with the water, salt and shoulder of lamb. Heat.

Carefully remove the froth that appears on the surface of the liquid and add the stock vegetables, bay leaves and peppers. Simmer, covered, for about two hours, until the meat is tender.

Remove the meat from the stock and sieve the liquid. Dice the meat into centimetre cubes. Pour the stock back into the saucepan and add the cabbage, cut into fine strips. Simmer for one hour and add the chopped carrots and diced potatoes, and the cubed shoulder of lamb and smoked lamb. Simmer until the potatoes are soft.

■ Add the parsley immediately before serving.

HERB-FLAVOURED CREAM CHEESE SOUP

■ Cook the chopped onion in butter until soft. Add the flour, and stew on a low heat for a couple of minutes.

    Add the heated stock and potato pieces. Heat to boiling point, whisking the soup until smooth. Simmer gently for 15–20 minutes. Pour the liquid into a liquidiser, liquidise well and season with salt.

■ In another pan, mix all the ingredients for finishing together thoroughly.

    Pour the hot soup over gradually, stirring strongly. Re-heat to close to boiling point, but do not allow to boil.

■ Take the soup off the heat and liquidise it again with a liquidiser or whisk. Serve at once.

4 SERVINGS

20 G BUTTER
1 ONION
20 G FLOUR
8 DL VEGETABLE STOCK
2 MEDIUM-SIZED POTATOES,
PEELED AND CUT INTO
FOUR PIECES
SALT

TO FINISH:

100 G CREAM CHEESE
2 EGG YOLKS
1/2 DL CREAM
2 TBSP FRESH CORIANDER,
CHOPPED
2 TBSP CHIVES, CHOPPED
1 TBSP DILL, CHOPPED
FRESHLY GROUND WHITE
PEPPER

4 SERVINGS

A 1–1 1/2 KG WHOLE
WHITEFISH, SCALES REMOVED
6 THIN, POSTCARD SIZED
PIECES OF PORK FAT
2 LARGE SPRIGS OF DILL

FOR THE PASTRY:

300 G RYE FLOUR
100 G WHEAT FLOUR
400 G FINE SALT
3 DL EGG WHITES
(8–10 EGGS)

FOR THE SAUCE:

1 SHALLOT CHOPPED
2 1/2 DL GOOD FISH STOCK
1/2 DL DRY WHITE WINE
2 DL WHIPPING CREAM
30 G BUTTER
1 TSP ANCHOVY, FINELY
CHOPPED, AND A LITTLE
ANCHOVY STOCK
2 TBSP CHOPPED DILL
BLACK PEPPER

WHITEFISH IN A DARK SALT-CRUST PASTRY

■ Make the pastry by mixing all the ingredients thoroughly. Wrap the dough in plastic film and put it in the refrigerator for about half an hour.

■ Wipe the whitefish dry, cut the fins and even up the tail with scissors. Remove the gills and wipe the blood away carefully. Spread the pork-fat out on a piece of greaseproof paper. Season the whitefish lightly with salt, put the dill inside the fish, place the fish on top of the pork-fat and wrap the fish in the pork-fat.

■ Roll the pastry out to a thickness of about half a centimetre, into a longish piece, and wrap it tightly around the whitefish. Salt-crust pastry forms seams easily.

■ Cook the chopped shallot with the fish stock and white wine until a syrupy mixture is formed. Add the cream and boil until the sauce begins to thicken. Add the butter. Add the anchovy and a little anchovy stock and liquidise the sauce in a liquidiser. Sieve it, and add the chopped dill and a little freshly ground black pepper.

■ Heat the oven to 230°C. Place the whitefish on baking paper on a baking tray and bake for 30 minutes. At the table, cut the top part of the pastry case open completely. Remove the 'lid' and the pieces of pork-fat.

■ Serve the fish, offering with it the anchovy sauce and boiled potatoes.

A good choice of wine would be a German Riesling from the Rheingau.

PIKE-PERCH WITH SMOKED SALMON AND HONEY SAUCE

■ Make a cut in the back of the pikeperch fillets with a sharp knife. Fill the cavity with the slices of smoked salmon. Season the fillets with ground white pepper. Mix the breadcrumbs with the flour and cover the fillets with the mixture.

■ Wash and slice the mushrooms. Cook the onions in butter until they are soft. Add the mushrooms to the pan and brown them lightly. Season with the salt, ground white pepper and soured cream.

■ Fry the pike-perch fillets in butter until done. Serve the creamed mushrooms on to plates and place the pike-perch fillets on top.

■ Put 2 tbsp butter and 1 tbsp honey into a frying pan and heat quickly. Pour the honey-butter on to the pike-perch fillets and serve at once.

The full flavours of this dish are well complemented by, for example, a Pouilly-Fuissé or a Gewürztraminer from Alsace.

4 SERVINGS

4 PIKE-PERCH FILLETS

120 G COLD-SMOKED SALMON
FILLETS IN SLICES

WHITE PEPPER

2 TBSP BREADCRUMBS

4 TBSP FLOUR

BUTTER FOR FRYING

FOR THE CREAMED MUSHROOMS:

300 G MUSHROOMS

4 TBSP ONIONS, CHOPPED

BUTTER FOR FRYING

SALT AND WHITE PEPPER

2 TBSP SOURED CREAM

FOR THE HONEY SAUCE:

2 TBSP BUTTER

1 TBSP HONEY

4 SERVINGS

4 WHITEFISH FILLETS, APPROXIMATELY 700 G IN TOTAL

WHITE PEPPER AND SALT

3 TBSP BUTTER

3–4 TBSP FINELY GROUND SOUR-DOUGH CRISPBREAD

FOR THE BEER SAUCE:

2 TBSP BUTTER

2 TBSP FLOUR

3 DL CREAM

SALT AND WHITE PEPPER

GROUND CARAWAY

1 DL BEER

1 DL WHIPPED CREAM

WHITEFISH FLAVOURED WITH SOUR-DOUGH BREAD AND BEER SAUCE

■ Season the whitefish fillets with the ground white pepper and salt. Place the fillets on a buttered oven-dish, skin up, and butter them with soft butter. Sprinkle the ground crispbread on top. Bake in the oven at 200°C for 10–15 minutes.

■ Melt the butter in a saucepan. Add the flour and mix until the consistency is even. Add the warm cream, the salt and pepper, and the chopped caraway. Simmer the sauce for 10 minutes on a medium heat, stirring from time to time. Add the beer and the whipped cream. Bring to the boil and serve at once.

■ Place the whitefish fillets on plates, pour the sauce liberally over, and serve with boiled potatoes.

Light wheat beer or mineral water are the best accompaniments to this dish.

PERCH FILLETS WITH MUSHROOM AND SWEETBREAD STUFFING

■ Remove all bones from the perch fillets. Season the fillets with salt and fry them quickly in butter. Set aside and keep warm. Handle the fillets with care, so that they do not break up.

■ Cut the ripe sweetbreads into small cubes.

■ To remove the poison, bring the morels to the boil at least twice in two different changes of water. Then fry the morels, leek and sweetbreads lightly in butter. Add the cream and simmer until the cream has thickened. Season with salt and pepper, add the dill. Add the prawns immediately before serving, so that they do not toughen.

■ Place on each plate, first, a perch fillet, inside uppermost. Place some hot stuffing on top and cover with a second fillet, outside uppermost. Decorate with dill and serve with boiled potatoes and vegetables.

A dry and strongly acidic Alsace Riesling is a good accompaniment to this dish.

4 SERVINGS

8 MEDIUM-SIZED PERCH FILLETS

SALT

100 G BUTTER

FOR THE STUFFING:

150 G RIPE SWEETBREADS

100 G MORELS, BLANCHED AT LEAST TWICE, CHOPPED

CHOPPED LEEK

30 G BUTTER

2 DL WHIPPING CREAM

SALT AND PEPPER FROM THE MILL

CHOPPED DILL

50 G PRAWNS, PEELED

4 SERVINGS

4 BONELESS CHICKEN BREASTS

400 G MUSHROOMS

1 LEEK

50 G BUTTER

2 DL CREAM

SALT AND WHITE PEPPER

CHICKEN BREAST STUFFED WITH MUSHROOMS

■ Slice the mushrooms and chop the leek. Glaze in the butter; add the cream and allow to thicken. Season with salt and pepper and allow to cool.

Cut a pocket in the chicken breasts between the inner and outer fillets. Pound the fillets lightly. Fill the pockets you have made with the mushroom–leek mixture and reshape the breasts to their original form. Fry in butter in a frying pan and, finally, season with salt and white pepper.

■ Serve with, for example, tomato rice.

A dry, slightly nutty white Burgundy, for example from Mâcon, provides a good complement to this dish.

LAMB TRIO

■ Boil the lamb's tongues in salted water until done. Remove the skin while still hot. Soak the lamb's kidneys for a moment in cold water.

■ Prepare the red wine sauce. Add the wine, roughly chopped shallots and herbs to the basic sauce. Finally, whisk in the cubed, cold butter. Heat, but do not allow to boil after the addition of the butter.

■ Fry the lamb chops and kidneys quickly so that they remain pink inside. Heat the tongues in their cooking liquid.

Add the rosemary to the sauce. Make a small pool of sauce on each plate, and place a chop, tongue and kidney on it.

■ Serve with, for example, ratatouille.

A successful wine choice might be, for example, a Spanish Cabernet Sauvignon from Penedés or an Australian Cabernet Sauvignon.

4 SERVINGS

4 LAMB'S TONGUES

WATER, SALT

4 LAMB'S KIDNEYS

4 LAMB CHOPS

FOR THE RED WINE SAUCE:

2 DL BROWN SAUCE

1 DL RED WINE

2 SHALLOTS

PARSLEY

60 G UNSALTED BUTTER

1 SPRIG OF ROSEMARY

4 SERVINGS

12 50 G SADDLES OF
COMPLETELY CLEANED LAMB
FILLET

12 SMALL, FINE SLICES OF
MILDLY SMOKED BACON

4 SHORT BAMBOO SKEWERS

BUTTER FOR FRYING

SALT AND PEPPER

FOR THE PANCAKES:

400 G PEELED POTATOES,
OF A FLOURY VARIETY

SALT, WATER

4 TBSP FLOUR

5 TBSP MILK

4 TBSP THICK CREAM

PEPPER

A LITTLE GRATED NUTMEG

CLEAR MELTED BUTTER
FOR FRYING

**FOR THE FETA
GRATIN:**

100 G FETA

100 G CREAM CHEESE

2 EGG YOLKS

1 TBSP SOURED CREAM

1/4 TSP COARSELY GROUND
BLACK PEPPER

1 TBSP CHIVES, CHOPPED

1 TBSP FRESH CORIANDER,

SADDLES OF LAMB ON A SPIT,
FETA PANCAKES

■ Shape the saddles to a thickness of around 1 1/2 cm and wrap the slices of bacon around them. Thread the saddles on to the skewers, three per skewer.

■ Boil the potatoes in a small amount of salted water and press them, while hot, through a sieve or food press. Immediately mix in the flour and boiled milk. Cover with a cloth and allow to cool completely.

Add the eggs one by one, whisking carefully. Finally, add the cream and season the batter. Make thickish pancakes using clear melted butter in a pancake pan.

■ Mix all the ingredients for the feta gratin in a food processor until they form a purée. Cover the pancakes with the mixture and grill them until the surface acquires a good colour.

■ Fry the saddles in a non-stick pan in a little butter. Season with salt and freshly ground pepper.

■ Place three feta pancakes and three saddles on each plate. Serve a red wine sauce separately.

Suitable wines include a medium-bodied and ample Médoc or a Tignanello from Tuscany.

MEDALLIONS OF PORK WITH BRIE AND BRAISED RED PEPPERS

■ Peel the peppers with a potato-peeler, cut them in two, remove all seeds and the pale part from the inside, cut into 3 cm pieces. Melt the butter in a saucepan and add the pieces of pepper. Braise, covered, on a medium heat for 10 minutes, stirring from time to time, until the peppers have softened slightly. Add both juices, the sugar and a little salt. Cover again and braise on a medium heat for 20 minutes, stirring occasionally. When the peppers are cooked, take the pan off the heat.

■ Mash the brie with a fork and mix it with the soft butter, the shallots, the paprika and the black pepper. Heat a non-stick frying pan, spread the bottom with butter and brown the pork medallions so that they remain a little raw at the centre. Set the medallions aside and season with salt. Heat the oven grill to 275°C. Set the medallions on a roasting tray. Divide the brie mixture into four parts. Shape the cheese mixture in the form of the medallion, and set it on top of the meat. Gratinate the medallions under the grill until the surface is brown.

■ Re-heat the paprika, spoon it on to plates and set a medallion on each plate.

A lightish, aromatic Beaujolais or a medium-bodied Côtes du Rhône is a good accompaniment to this dish.

4 SERVINGS

4 140 G MEDALLIONS OF LEAN PORK FILLET

150 G BRIE

1 TBSP SOFT BUTTER

2 SHALLOTS, VERY FINELY CHOPPED

1 TSP GROUND PAPRIKA

1/4 TSP COARSELY GROUND BLACK PEPPER

BUTTER FOR FRYING

SALT

FOR THE BRAISED PEPPERS:

2 LARGE RED PEPPERS

1 TBSP BUTTER

3 TBSP ORANGE JUICE

1 TBSP LEMON JUICE

1 TSP SUGAR

FOR THE PIE BASE:

2 EGGS

200 G CASTER SUGAR

1 DL MILK

1 DL WHIPPING CREAM

1 DL MELTED BUTTER

2 TSP BAKING POWDER

4 DL FLOUR

FOR THE FILLING:

1/2 L PEELED, CHOPPED RHUBARB

50 G SOFT BUTTER

100 G CASTER SUGAR

1 DL FLOUR

RHUBARB PIE

■ Heat the oven to 200°C.

Grease a rectangular baking tray — to which the dough will not stick — with a fine layer of butter, or place baking paper on an ordinary baking tray.

Mix the eggs and sugar carefully together. Add the milk, cream and melted butter; combine. Mix the baking powder and flour together. Add this mixture to the liquid, mixing it only just enough to achieve an even consistency. Spread the dough on the baking tray.

Place the pieces of rhubarb evenly on the dough. Rub the butter into the sugar and flour to form a crumbly consistency and sprinkle on top of the pie. Put the tray in the oven and bake for 25—30 minutes.

■ Serve with whipped cream or vanilla sauce.

RHUBARB
COOKED IN GRENADINE SYRUP

■ Peel the rhubarb, cut it diagonally into matchstick-sized pieces and place in a wide pan or a casserole with a lid.

Boil the water and the sugar together for 2–3 minutes, add the grenadine, and pour the boiling liquid over the rhubarb. Cover and simmer gently without mixing until the rhubarb has softened slightly. Cool the rhubarb in its liquid. Be careful not to cook the rhubarb for too long or on too high a heat, so that it does not break up.

The rhubarb can also be cooked in the oven. Heat the oven to 225°C. Put the lid on the casserole as soon as you have poured the boiling liquid over the rhubarb and put it in the oven immediately. Bake for 6–10 minutes and let the rhubarb cool in its liquid.

■ Serve with vanilla ice-cream and garnish the plates with, for example, a couple of fresh strawberries.

4 SERVINGS

500–600 G YOUNG RHUBARB

1/2 L WATER

200 G SUGAR

2–3 TBSP GRENADINE SYRUP

SUMMER

SUMMER

STARTS

ON THE FIRST

OF JUNE

The Finnish summer is short, but all the more intense for that. And its arrival is almost always a surprise. One morning, you open your eyes and realise it has come. Now and then it begins as early as May, but it generally arrives a little later.

At midsummer, the sun does not set at all. North of the Arctic Circle, it remains visible throughout the night, and even in the south it only dips beneath the horizon for a moment. In Lapland, the nightless night lasts for as long as 70 days.

The weekend after the summer solstice, midsummer is celebrated, the festival of the white nights. The blue-and-white Finnish flag is flown and, on the lake- and sea-shores, tens of thousands of midsummer bonfires are lit.

It is estimated that there are more than 400,000 summer cottages in Finland, and at least as many shore saunas. But there are few from which, on midsummer eve, the joyful hiss of water on hot stones and the powerful slap of bunches of fresh birch twigs cannot be heard. On the sauna stove a length of sausage sizzles

THERE IS NOTHING BETTER THAN FISH YOU HAVE CAUGHT YOURSELF. EXCEPT THE ONE THAT GOT AWAY

Someone has counted the lakes of Finland and reached the figure 187,888. The Finnish coastline is 1,100 kilometres long, and it is fringed with 80,000 islands. For almost all Finns, Sunday fishing — with rod and line, of course, above all — is a familiar activity from childhood.

When the fisherman feels a tugging on his line and the float bobs beneath the water's surface, there is probably a perch on the line.

The perch is the Finnish national fish, and the commonest edible fish of our inland waterways. Although perch may be caught all year round it is, many people believe, at its best in summer. The perch is mild and extraordinarily delicate in flavour.

And its flavour comes into its own through many different modes of cooking: fried, cooked on charcoal, freshly smoked or in the traditional fish soup. The authentic Savo *kalakukko* pie, too, is filled with little perches. Perch stock, too, makes an excellent basis for various sauces and soups.

The pike is a sizeable fish. It is said that the largest female pike ever caught measured 175 cm in length and weighed more than 25 kilograms. And what must the pike have weighed on whose jawbone Väinämöinen, the hero of the *Kalevala*, played his music? Fortunately, the individuals caught on line or net today are a little smaller. Pike are, indeed, at their most flavoursome at a weight of 1–2 kilograms.

Sometimes also called the shore pirate, the pike is the greediest creature in Finnish waters, a predatory fish that will eat almost anything. Finns have, nevertheless, invented a way of punishing this fellow by first boiling it whole and then enjoying it with white sauce and chopped, hard-boiled egg.

Pike are caught almost everywhere in the country, in both lakes and the archipelago waters of the Gulf of Finland and the Gulf of Bothnia. The Finnish pike — like the perch — has already made its way on to European dining tables. Its firm flesh is particularly suitable as a base for the various fish terrines. So, next time you order *Quenelles au gratin* in a Brussels or Lyons restaurant, you may well be served the Finnish shore pirate, in a particularly delicious form.

in its roasting-bag, and on the table of the sauna room waits a whitefish cooked on charcoal, taken from the net only a short while ago. The Finn is in his element.

THE WHITE NIGHTS WORK WONDERS

By midsummer, the long, light days have ripened the first vegetables: new potatoes, radishes, carrots, cucumbers and tomatoes. Garden strawberries grow redder and sweeter day by day. In the fields, wild strawberries gather delicious aromas.

The arrival of new potatoes in the markets is always one of the high points of the summer, and their flavour improves day by day. The herring fishermen, too, return from the Icelandic waters with their fresh catches, just in time for the arrival of the new potatoes.

Photo: Asko Hämäläinen/LKA

MUTTON AND CABBAGE FIND ONE ANOTHER

Finnish mutton is good, but unfortunately Finns themselves eat it far too seldom. If everyone still remembered how good the combination of young lamb and the first cabbage of spring is, lamb farmers would have no worries!

Finnish cabbage soup was originally made simply from shoulder or breast of lamb and fresh cabbage, seasoned with a little marjoram, salt and allspice. But the soup makes no objection if carrot and parsnip, for example, are added.

The Finnish housewife has borrowed the recipe for baked mutton cabbage from the cookbooks of our western neighbour, but mutton stew or thick mutton soup – which does not, however, contain cabbage – is known in Sweden by the name of Finnish mutton stew. This excellent stew is very reminiscent of the famous Irish stew, but contains more root vegetables.

Even a short eulogy of mutton cannot omit to mention roast lamb. This delicacy, smoked in the sauna in the manner of western Finland, is, fortunately, also available in the shops at times other than Easter.

HALF A MILLION MILK-PRODUCERS STROLL THROUGH THE SUMMER MEADOWS

Finland is a land of animal husbandry. The raising of dairy cattle and the production of milk represent as much as two thirds of the total agricultural produce of Finland. Finns drink most of their milk as such, or eat it in the form of cheese, butter or yoghurt. Finnish butter and, in particular, Finnish Emmenthal cheese, are well-known abroad. Less familiar, possibly, are *viili* (clabbered milk) and *piimä* (buttermilk).

Home-made *viili* is, especially for city-dwellers, a summer speciality, for new milk, warm from the cow, is required to make it. Milk and a dash of sour cream are poured into an individual-portion bowl in the form of a truncated cone and left in a warm, draught-free place to sour. The *viili* is ready in about 24 hours.

Before serving, it is cooled well, and is then enjoyed with fresh berries or sugar and cinnamon. Another accompaniment is *talkkuna* – a fine powder made of milled oats, barley and peas which, mixed with *viili*, transforms it into a nourishing meal.

Industrially produced *viili* is still a common breakfast dish and snack today. Cream *viili*, made from soured cream, is the basis for the Finns' favourite salad dressings.

Visit a summer festival and the many cheerful Finnish summer markets

If the sheer number of festivals and summer events is anything to go by, Finns' hunger for culture increases as the days grow longer. And cultural events offer an opportunity to strike up an acquaintance with the gastronomic cultures of the different provinces.

Visiting local markets gives the best general impression of the province's most typical products and culinary specialities. At midsummer, the markets are at their busiest, and local produce is on show in greater abundance than at any other time of year. And more: one always meets interesting people at markets.

Markets have long since given up their role as providers of essential everyday foodstuffs; that function has been taken over by the supermarkets and large department stores.

Perhaps it is for this very reason that the summer market is filled with such an unhurried and amiable atmosphere.

Aqua vitae, the water of life in the Finnish manner

It is said that the Finnish national poet, Johan Ludvig Runeberg, once opined that a tot of liquor was to be enjoyed only with fish dishes. A practical man, he nevertheless added: 'If no decent fish is available, pancakes can also be considered fish.'

The world has changed since Runeberg's time. Today we raise a frosted glass much more seldom than in past decades, but for many Finns it is still an indispensable part of many festive ceremonies. And the cause for celebration need be no greater than, for example, the new herring, the first morels of spring, the opening of the crayfish season or catching one's own salmon. And to eat the salt cod of Christmas without the requisite dram could be considered almost insulting to that fine fish, some people say.

The poet Runeberg's drams in the first half of the 19th century were probably flavourless liquor distilled from grain. The secrets of its preparation had travelled westwards with soldiers a little more than a hundred years before – and from where else but Russia.

Flavoured liquor arrived in Finland as the 19th century prog-

ressed. The use of spices and herbs was learned primarily from Sweden, but the Danes, too, may have had a say in the matter.

Bitter orange, caraway, aniseed and fennel gradually became established as flavourings for commercial products, while individual recipes were developed from berries and natural herbs for home distilling.

As we know, the French call all drinks distilled from wine *Eau de vie*. And it was not long before the Scandinavians began to use the same name of their own grain-distilled and flavoured liquors. The very same that is now known the world over as *aquvavit*.

Finnish vodka is the best in the world, many people say, and not only Finns. We shall not dispute matters of taste, but Finnish liquors are certainly also excellent when flavoured. For schnapps flavoured in the Russian manner, experts recommend Koskenkorva liquor, which contains a little sugar, in place of ordinary vodka. The flavour can be further rounded by the addition of syrup (one part sugar and one part water are brought to the boil and cooled before use).

Your health!

Bog myrtle (Myrica gale)

■ A bush that blooms in the marshes in May, whose leaves give a pale yellow schnapps. A couple of hundred leaves are needed for a bottle of vodka. After macerating for a week, the drink is sieved and left to mature for at least 2–3 months.

St John's-wort (Hypericum maculatum)

■ A herb that flowers at midsummer, whose yellow flowers give a strong extract of a fine red colour. Around 1 dl of flowers are needed for a bottle of vodka. The extract is ready in about a week, after which it is sieved. This strong-tasting schnapps can easily be diluted.

WORMWOOD (ARTEMISIA ABSINTHIUM)

An ancient Egyptian herb which has been used to repel insects and as a remedy for malaria and cholera, the herb's Latin name implies, its distilled oil was also used as an active ingredient in the notorious absinthe.

The grass should be picked in early summer, before flowering, and dried carefully to remove the oil. Five or six sprigs are ample to flavour a bottle of vodka in a couple of days. After this, the pale yellow liquid is sieved and diluted to taste.

BLACKCURRANT (RIBES NIGRUM)

To make blackcurrant liquor, 3–5 dl of ripe, fresh blackcurrants are needed per bottle, and a couple of blackcurrant leaves, if a stronger flavour is desired. The drink should mature for 4–6 months, after which it is sieved carefully, without squashing the berries.

Rowan-berry liquor is prepared by soaking the berries bitten by the first frost in vodka for about a month. The drink is sieved and stored away. The sediment that gathers in the bottle is sieved away, and the drink is diluted when necessary with fresh vodka.

1.	BLACKCURRANT VODKA
2.	FINLANDIA VODKA
3.	WORMWOOD VODKA
4.	PEPPER VODKA
5.	EXTRA-AQUAVIT
6.	SAVON WIINA (SCHNAPPS FROM SAVO)
7.	KOSKENKORVAN VIINA (KOSKENKORVA SCHNAPPS)
8.	BOG MYRTLE VODKA
9.	ZUBROWKA VODKA
10.	MUSHROOM VODKA
11.	MANNERHEIM'S SHOT
12.	ST.JOHN'S-WORT VODKA

week at room temperature in a darkened place for about a week. Drink chilled.

MUSHROOM VODKA

■ As above, but add a few dried horn-of-plenty mushrooms instead of the zubrowka.

LEMON VODKA

Grate the rind of a lemon (do not include any of the pith) and mix it with 6 ml of sugar syrup. Pour into a bottle of Koskenkorva vodka and allow to mature at room temperature for a week. Sieve, cool and serve.

MANNERHEIM'S SHOT

■ In addition to his career as a soldier and statesman, the Marshal of Finland, Carl Gustav Mannerheim, was known as a true gourmet. The cocktail known as Mannerheim's shot originated in his wartime headquarters in Mikkeli.

■ The drink is chilled and glasses are filled to the brim. Mannerheim was known for his unusually steady hands.

The Mikkeli Club still serves the Marshal's shots mixed according to the original recipe.

FLAVOURED VODKA IN THE RUSSIAN STYLE

PEPPER VODKA

■ To a litre bottle of Koskenkorva vodka add 6 ml syrup, 10 white peppercorns, 10 black peppercorns and 10 green peppercorns. Mix and allow to stand at room temperature in a darkened place for about a week. Drink chilled.

ZUBROWKA VODKA

■ To a bottle of Koskenkorva add 6 ml syrup and three blades of zubrowka or holy grass (*Hierocloë odorata*). Allow to stand for a

AN ADVENTURE IN THE SUMMER ARCHIPELAGO IN THE COMPANY OF BALTIC HERRING, HERRING AND A LITTLE FRESH-SALTED WHITEFISH

It came by sea a couple of hundred years ago from Sweden. Now it makes the return journey to Stockholm from Helsinki and Turku – every evening at exactly the same time.

It is, of course, the *smörgåsbord*, which has since become the Finnish buffet table and, through the decades, the greatest and most spectacular sight of the ferries that ply back and forth between Finland and Sweden. The white- and red-sided ships have, through the years, grown to the size of apartment blocks, but the buffet tables remain the same. As has the summer archipelago of the Gulf of Finland. It is a combination with which

1.	FRIED AND GRILLED BALTIC HERRINGS MARINADED IN
	A VINEGAR SAUCE
2.	GLASS MASTER'S HERRING
3.	SPICED BALTIC HERRING
4.	SMOKED BALTIC HERRING
5.	BALTIC HERRING PATTIES MARINATED IN VINEGAR
6.	HERBED BALTIC HERRING
7.	COBBLER'S SALMON
8.	HERRING IN SOURED CREAM
9.	WARM-SMOKED WHITEFISH, RAINBOW TROUT AND EEL
10.	BROILED SALMON FINS
11.	COLD-SMOKED RAINBOW TROUT
12.	FRESH-SALTED WHITEFISH
13.	RUSSIAN HERRING
14.	MUSTARD SAUCE

few panoramic restaurants in the world can compete.

You can experience the atmosphere of the archipelago at its most authentic on the deck of an old yawl or fishing schooner. In Helsinki's north harbour, for example, there floats a little flotilla of these wooden sailing boats, lovingly restored. Most of them can be hired for an hour or two or for a whole day, and they have room for dozens of friends of the herring.

IN PRAISE OF HERRING

An orthodox buffet table, of course, includes much more than Baltic herring, herring and salted fish, but Baltic herring and herring are the heart and soul of an authentic buffet table.

Originally, everything offered on the table was made of herring and Baltic herring, variously prepared. Not without good reason did our neighbours the Swedes call it the salt table (*saltbord*). Even more generally, it was known by the name of liquor table (*brännvinsbord*). For it was the custom for the table to be crowned by a centrepiece consisting of a silver liquor fountain with six taps from which each guest could pour a few drops of his favourite schnapps to wash down the fish. And all this was just a light hors d'oeuvre before sitting down at the dining table.

Allhonour to the herring, which comes to our tables from the northerly waters of Iceland and Norway. Although the Baltic herring is only a minor second cousin, it has, as a native of the Baltic, always played a role out of all proportion to its size in the cuisine of the Finns.

Just like the herring, the Baltic herring is at home in the same vinegar-based marinades. It makes excellent fresh-salted fish, and it is traditionally also marinated when fried, charcoal grilled and smoked. And it is made into an anchovy preserve, an important ingredient in "Jansson's temptation", which also includes potatoes, onions and cream..

Baltic herring is a cheap fish. It would not be unreasonable to argue that it is in part on its strength that the Finnish people have survived the many hard times of their history. It is perhaps for this reason that the Baltic herring is still not valued as a 'dinner-table fish' to the extent it deserves. Fortunately, the old attitudes are gradually crumbling. With a little imagination and the ingredients of 'elegant' fish recipes, the Baltic herring can be transformed into wonderfully tasty and impressive dishes, which can already be found on the menus of our best restaurants.

TERHENIEMI HERRING IN SOURED CREAM

400 G HERRING FILLETS, SOAKED	
I ONION	
2–3 DL SOURED CREAM	
2 TBSP CHOPPED DILL	
FRESHLY GROUND WHITE PEPPER	

■ Cut the herring fillets into 1/2 cm slices. Slice the onion. Place all the ingredients in a glass jar so that there are three layers of each ingredient, and the top layer is of soured cream. Seal the jar well and let the herring macerate for at least 24 hours.

SLIGHTLY SALTED WHITEFISH

4 SERVINGS	FOR THE MUSTARD SAUCE:
	2 1/2 DL MUSTARD
2 WHITEFISH FILLETS	3 TBSP CASTER SUGAR
I TBSP COARSE SALT	3–4 TBSP WHITE WINE VINEGAR
SUGAR	SALT AND GROUND WHITE PEPPER
FRESHLY GROUND WHITE PEPPER	1/2 DL MAIZE OR SUNFLOWER OIL
CHOPPED DILL	1–2 TBSP CHOPPED DILL

■ Carefully remove all the bones from the whitefish fillets. Place them side by side in a shallow dish, skin side down, and spread with the salt, sugar, white pepper and chopped dill.

Cover the dish and place in the refrigerator for about an hour to macerate.

■ Mix together the mustard, sugar, white wine vinegar, salt and pepper. Allow to stand for a moment, until the sugar has dissolved. Slowly whisk in the oil, as if you were making a mayonnaise. Keep in a sealed container.

■ Before serving, remove the superfluous salt and seasoning from the surfaces of the fillets and cut them along the skin into very fine slices using a fillet knife. Serve with the mustard sauce.

RUSSIAN HERRING

4–6 SERVINGS
400 G HERRING FILLETS,
SOAKED IN WATER
1 BEETROOT
100 G PICKLED CUCUMBERS
1 ONION
2 HARD-BOILED EGGS
50 G CAPERS

■ Cut the beetroot, pickled cucumber and onion into small cubes. Cut the herring fillets into 1 cm slices. Separate the egg whites from the yolks and chop both into very small cubes.

■ Place the chopped herring fillet in the middle of a serving dish and, around it in separate piles, set the chopped onion, beetroot, pickled cucumber, egg yolks and whites and the capers. Serve with soured cream that has been stirred until it is runny.

COBBLER'S SALMON

	For the marinade:
1 KG SALTED BALTIC HERRING	3 DL WATER
1–2 ONIONS, CHOPPED	3 DL SUGAR
A FEW SPRIGS OF DILL	3 DL LIQUOR VINEGAR
	2 BAY LEAVES
	5 ALLSPICE PEPPERCORNS

■ Soak the Baltic herrings in cold water for a couple of hours.

Clean the Baltic herrings and remove the bones. Roll them up, skin side out, and pile them into a dish or glass jar, layering them with the onion and sprigs of dill. Mix the ingredients of the sauce together, bring to the boil and allow to cool a little. Pour the sauce over the Baltic herrings and macerate in a cold place for 3 to 4 days.

'GRAYFISH' BALTIC HERRING

10 SERVINGS	2 TBSP OIL
	1 TBSP WHITE WINE VINEGAR
1.2 KG BALTIC HERRING FILLETS	2 TBSP CASTER SUGAR
2 TBSP FINELY CHOPPED DILL (THE CROWNS	WATER
OF LATE SUMMER DILL, IF POSSIBLE)	12 ALLSPICE PEPPERCORNS
SALT	12 WHITE PEPPERCORNS
1 1/2 DL TOMATO PURÉE	1 ONION, FINELY CHOPPED

■ Grease a suitable shallow oven dish with oil and sprinkle the chopped dill on the base. Season the Baltic herring fillets with salt and roll them up tightly, skin side upward. Place the rolls in the dish.

Mix the oil, vinegar, sugar and a little salt with the tomato purée. Thin the sauce to a suitable consistency with water. Spread it over the Baltic herring rolls and sprinkle the coarsely ground peppercorns and very finely chopped onion over. Bake for 25 minutes in a 225 °C oven.

■ This dish is excellent hot, but is usually served cold the next day.

MACERATED BRAISED AND GRILLED BALTIC HERRINGS

	For the marinade:
1 KG WHOLE BALTIC HERRINGS,	1 CARROT, 1 ONION
GUTTED AND CLEANED	
SALT AND WHITE PEPPER	1 1/2 DL LIQUOR VINEGAR
2 TBSP BREADCRUMBS	1 1/2 DL SUGAR, 3 DL WATER
1 TBSP FLOUR	10 WHOLE ALLSPICE PEPPERCORNS
BUTTER FOR FRYING	4 BAY LEAVES

■ Rinse the Baltic herrings quickly in cold water and dry them well with kitchen paper. Season half the herrings with salt and ground white pepper. Mix the flour and the breadcrumbs and carefully roll the seasoned herrings in the mixture. Fry in butter until done. Braise the rest of the herrings on a very hot, salted baking tray or frying pan. Place the herrings in two shallow dishes.

■ Cut the peeled carrot into slices and the onion into strips. Put all the ingredients in a steel saucepan, bring to the boil and allow to cool. Pour the liquid over the herrings, cover the dishes carefully and allow the herrings to macerate in a cold place for 24 hours.

8—10 SERVINGS

1 KG SALMON FILLET, FROM

THE MIDDLE OF THE FISH

3 TBSP SEA SALT

1 TBSP FINE SALT

3 TBSP CASTER SUGAR

1 DL DRIED FENNEL

1 DL DRIED DILL

10 WHOLE WHITE

PEPPERCORNS

FOR THE MUSTARD
SAUCE:

2 TBSP DIJON MUSTARD

2 TBSP ORDINARY MUSTARD

2 TBSP WHITE WINE VINEGAR

2 DL OIL

SALT AND WHITE PEPPER

DILL-FENNEL SALMON
WITH MUSTARD SAUCE

■ Remove all the bones from the salmon fillet. Mix the salts and the sugar and, in a separate bowl, the fennel and the dill. Place the fish in a salting dish, skin side down. Rub the fish all over with the sugar-salt mixture. Add the coarsely ground white peppercorns and cover the whole fillet with the fennel-dill mixture. Macerate for 24 hours.

■ Put the mustards and the sugar in a bowl and mix well. Add the white wine vinegar and whisk in the oil, a few drops at a time. Add salt and white pepper according to taste.

■ Take the fillet from the cold just before serving. Leave the herbs on the surface of the fish. Cut the seasoned fillet diagonally into narrow strips.

■ Serve with the mustard sauce and, for example, dark bread, beer and chilled schnapps.

TOMATO BAVAROIS FLAVOURED WITH CARAWAY

4–6 SERVINGS

■ Remove the tops from the tomatoes, cut a cross on top and place them in vigorously boiling water for 10 seconds. Lift them out and place immediately in iced water, cool and peel. Cut the tomatoes open, remove the flesh and cut into small pieces.

Melt the butter and add the chopped shallot, the crushed garlic clove and the caraway. Cook until the onion is soft. Add the tomato purée and boil, covered, for about 20 minutes. Season with salt, black pepper and sugar. Liquidise the mixture to a fine consistency in a food processor.

Mix the tomato sauce with the egg yolks and thicken a little in a bain marie.

While the tomatoes are cooking, soak the gelatine leaves in cold water. Add them to the hot tomato sauce and allow the sauce to cool gradually to room temperature, stirring occasionally. Whip the sour cream and mix it carefully with the tomato sauce. Place the mixture immediately in 1 1/2 dl timbale dishes, cover with kitchen film and chill in the refrigerator until firm.

■ Turn out the bavarois and garnish them with lettuce leaves and dill tops, soured cream and a few capers.

800 RIPE RED TOMATOES
2 TBSP BUTTER
50 G SHALLOTS, CHOPPED
1 SMALL CLOVE OF GARLIC
1/2 TSP CARAWAY, POUNDED IN A MORTAR
2 TSP TOMATO PURÉE
SALT AND FRESHLY GROUND BLACK PEPPER
1–2 TSP CASTER SUGAR
2 EGG YOLKS
2 LEAVES GELATINE
2 DL SOURED CREAM OR SOUR CREAM
LETTUCE LEAVES, DILL TOPS AND CAPERS TO GARNISH

6 SERVINGS	

FOR THE STOCK:

500 G SMALL PERCH, CLEANED, AND WITH GILLS REMOVED

500 G PERCH BONES

1 1/2 L WATER

100 G ONIONS

100 G LEEKS

2 SPRIGS OF PARSLEY

1 SPRIG OF DILL

HALF A BAY LEAF

5 ALLSPICE PEPPERCORNS

5 WHITE PEPPERCORNS

FOR THE SOUP VEGETABLES AND FINISHING:

150 G PERCH FILLETS

7 1/2 DL PERCH STOCK

50 G ONION, CHOPPED

50 G SMALL CAULIFLOWER FLORETS

50 G CARROTS, DICED TO THE SIZE OF A LITTLE FINGER-TIP

50 G PEAS, FRESH OR FROZEN

SEA SALT

1/2 L MILK

30 G BUTTER

1 TBSP CHIVES, CHOPPED

PERCH FILLETS AND VEGETABLES IN THE STYLE OF THE TRADITIONAL SUMMER SOUP

■ Cut up the perch and bones, rinse well and place in a saucepan. Add around 1 1/2 l water. Bring rapidly to the boil. Then turn down the heat so that the stock simmers gently, and remove the froth that forms on the surface.

Add the root vegetables, onions and spices, cook for 25 minutes and sieve the stock. Measure its volume: you need 7 1/2 dl. If there is more stock, reduce it.

■ Put all the vegetables in the stock, season with sea salt, and cook until done. Add the perch fillets, cut into 2 cm pieces, and the milk. Bring to the boil.

■ Check the seasoning and, finally, add the butter and the chopped chives. Serve the soup immediately.

The best accompaniment to this dish is mineral water. Or — why not? — a medium dry white wine.

PERCH CONSOMMÉ WITH CRAYFISH RAVIOLI

■ Rinse the cleaned perch and place in cold water. Bring to the boil. Remove the foam. Add the stock vegetables and seasonings. Simmer gently for about 35 minutes. Sieve the stock and allow to cool. Mix the vegetables with the egg whites and add to the stock, stirring until the whites have solidified. Leave the stock to stand for a moment before sieving. Strain the stock through a sieve. Cut the leek and carrot into fine strips. Add the strips to the stock and bring to the boil.

■ Place the flour on a working surface. Make a well in the centre and pour in the egg and oil. Mix to form a dough and knead. Wrap the dough in kitchen film and set to rest for half an hour. Start making the stuffing by cutting the vegetables into very small cubes (brunoise). Glaze them in butter until soft. Season with salt and pepper and allow to cool. Roll the dough out into two thin sheets and brush them with egg. Place the cubed vegetables on one of the sheets in four small piles. Cut the crayfish tails in half lengthwise and place them on top of the vegetables. Place the other sheet of dough on top and use a pasta mould to make four ravioli about 5 cm in diameter. Seal the edges of the ravioli well and boil in salted water for about 3 minutes. Place the ravioli in soup plates and pour the perch consommé over.

4 SERVINGS

2 KG FRESH, CLEANED PERCH

2 ONIONS

2 CARROTS, 1 LEEK

A BAY LEAF, SALT

WHITE AND BLACK PEPPER

SPRIGS OF DILL

TO CLARIFY:

RAW ROOT VEGETABLES

(CARROT, ONION, PARSNIP),

CUT VERY FINE

5 EGG WHITES

FOR THE CRAYFISH RAVIOLI:

PASTA DOUGH:

100 G COARSISH FLOUR

1 EGG

1 TBSP OIL

1 EGG FOR SEALING

FILLING:

A SMALL CARROT

A PIECE OF LEEK AND CELERY

BUTTER

8 CRAYFISH TAILS

SALT AND WHITE PEPPER

12 THIN, EQUAL-SIZED SLICES OF RAINBOW TROUT OF 50 G EACH

80 G SOFTENED BUTTER

1 TSP FRENCH MUSTARD

20 G GRATED HORSERADISH

A FEW DROPS OF LEMON JUICE

BLACK PEPPER

SALT

40 VERY FINE SLICES FROM A SMALL CUCUMBER

SEA SALT

WATER

RAINBOW TROUT
WITH CUCUMBER AND HORSERADISH

■ Cream the butter until pale, add the mustard, grated horseradish, lemon juice and a little freshly ground pepper.

Butter a shallow oven dish and sprinkle a little salt on its base.

Make four fans of three pieces of rainbow trout each. Spread the fans evenly with the horseradish butter.

Blanch the cucumber slices in vigorously boiling salted water for 30 seconds, cool immediately in iced water and dry well. Place the cucumber slices on the fans, overlapping evenly like fish scales, beginning from the narrowest point of the fan. Add 3 tbsp water to the dish and cover tightly with aluminium foil. Heat the oven to 200°C and cook the fans for 8 minutes.

■ Before serving, grind a little sea salt over the cucumber slices. Serve alone, or with good mashed potatoes.

A very dry, fruity white wine makes a good accompaniment, for example Muscadet or an American Fumé Blanc.

SALMON AND PERCH TART

■ Wash and blanch the spinach in vigorously boiling water for 2 minutes. Cool in cold water and squeeze the water out thoroughly. Cook the chopped onion in 80 g of the butter. Add the mushrooms and fry until the liquid has evaporated. Add the spinach and heat well; season with salt, pepper and nutmeg. Set to one side and allow to cool. Cut the perch fillets into small cubes, season with salt, pepper and nutmeg. Put in a cold place for 10 minutes. Purée the cubes in a food processor, adding the egg whites one by one. Finally, slowly pour in the cream. Season.

■ Butter a 24–26 cm diameter cake-tin with the remaining butter. Spread the spinach mixture evenly over the base of the tin, pressing it down. Pipe half of the perch mixture over the spinach and smooth. Place all the salmon slices evenly on the mixture and season with salt and pepper. Pipe the rest of the perch mixture over the salmon and smooth. Heat the oven to 170°C. Cover the cake-tin with buttered aluminium foil. Place the tin in a deep baking dish and pour in water at 70°C to a depth of 3 cm. Bake in this bain marie for 50–60 minutes. When the tart is ready, loosen its sides with a knife and turn the tart out on to a serving dish. Serve the tart with a fresh tomatoes, white wine- or shrimp sauce.

Wine: a dry and acidic Pouilly-Vinzelles or a Pinot Blanc from Alsace.

8—10 SERVINGS

500 G PERCH FILLETS
500 G FINE SLICES OF SALMON
600 G FRESH SPINACH
WATER
1 MEDIUM ONION, CHOPPED
100 G BUTTER
200 G FRESH MUSHROOMS, SLICED
SALT, PEPPER, NUTMEG
3 EGG WHITES
4 DL THICK CREAM

4 SERVINGS	FOR THE BEETROOT SAUCE:
700 G PIKE FILLETS	400 G BEETROOT, BOILED IN
2 DL SOURED CREAM	ITS SKIN
1/2 TSP COARSELY GROUND	2 DL WHITE WINE
BLACK PEPPER	2 DL FISH STOCK
3 TBSP BREADCRUMBS	1 TBSP LEMON JUICE
1 TBSP FLOUR	SALT AND WHITE PEPPER
1 TBSP DILL, CHOPPED	1 TBSP BUTTER
1/2 TSP SALT	

PIKE MACERATED IN SOURED CREAM WITH BEETROOT SAUCE

■ Dry the pike fillets with kitchen roll. Mix the coarsely ground black pepper with the soured cream and spread the mixture evenly over the surface of the fillets, on both sides. Allow to macerate in a cold place for at least four hours.

Mix the flour and dill with the breadcrumbs. Place the pike fillets on a buttered baking tray and sprinkle the breadcrumb mixture evenly over them. Cook in a 200 °C oven for 15–20 minutes, until the surface is a handsome brown in colour.

■ Peel the beetroot and cut into small pieces. Bring the white wine, fish stock and lemon juice to the boil. Add the beetroot and bring to the boil again. Liquidise the sauce carefully, and season with salt and finely ground white pepper. Finally, whisk the butter into the sauce.

■ Make a pool of sauce on each plate and place a pike fillet on it. Garnish with sprigs of dill and chopped chives. Serve with boiled potatoes.

A Chardonnay from Burgundy or a white Rioja would make a good accompaniment to this dish.

ROULADE OF WHITEFISH WITH CHIVE SAUCE

■ Season the fish with salt. Form the fillets into loose rolls, with the skin facing outward. Secure the rolls with a toothpick or put them on a skewer. Place the rolls in a smoking tray on a greased wire tray. Place 1 dl of alder chips, a juniper branch and ten juniper berries on the bottom of the smoking tray. Smoke for about 10 minutes at a medium heat.

■ Put the wine vinegar, water, wine and shallot in a saucepan. Simmer until the mixture is reduced by half in volume. Whisk in the butter in small cubes. Heat again, but do not allow to boil. Season with the salt, pepper and lemon. Add the cream and, finally, the chopped chives.

■ Make a pool of sauce on each plate and place a smoked whitefish roulade at its centre. You can also fill the roulade with, for example, a purée of vegetables.

The combination of flavours is complemented by a Gewürztraminer or Pinot Gris from Alsace.

4	SERVINGS

4 WHITEFISH FILLETS, AROUND 600 G IN TOTAL

SALT

OIL FOR GREASING

FOR THE CHIVE SAUCE:

1/2 DL WHITE WINE VINEGAR

1/2 DL WATER

1 DL DRY WHITE WINE

2 TBSP SHALLOTS, FINELY CHOPPED

100 G BUTTER

SALT AND WHITE PEPPER

1 TSP LEMON JUICE

2 TBSP WHIPPING CREAM

A BUNCH OF CHIVES

4 SERVINGS

	FOR THE KOHLRABI WITH BLACK PEPPER-CORNS:
4 FILLET STEAKS, 180 G EACH	400 G KOHLRABI, PEELED
IN WEIGHT	100 G ONION, CHOPPED
3 DL FRESH RYE BREAD,	WATER
GRATED	SALT
12 BLACK PEPPERS, CRUSHED	2 TBSP BUTTER, CREAMED
1 TBSP CHIVES, CHOPPED	2 TSP BLACK PEPPER,
1 TBSP PARSLEY, TORN	COARSELY GROUND
1 CLOVE GARLIC, CHOPPED	
4 TBSP SOURED CREAM	
1 TSP ANCHOVIES, CHOPPED	
SALT AND PEPPER	
2 TBSP BUTTER FOR FRYING	

STEAK WITH SOUR-DOUGH BREAD GRATIN

■ Cut the kohlrabi into 1/2 cm cubes and boil in salted water with the chopped onion until just tender. Drain and keep warm.

■ Mix the ground peppercorns, chives, parsley, garlic, soured cream and anchovies with the grated bread. Season the steaks with salt and pepper. Brown them quickly in a little butter, leaving them distinctly raw inside. Take the steaks from the pan, allow them to cool for a moment and spread the gratin mixture evenly all over the surface of the steaks. Finish the steaks under a grill or using the grill setting of the oven. Mix the creamed butter with the kohlrabi just before serving.

■ Place the steaks on plates and make a neat pile of kohlrabi next to each one. Sprinkle ground black pepper over the kohlrabi.

A good choice of wine would be a Côtes du Rhône or a Californian Cabernet Sauvignon.

LAMB AND CABBAGE PIE

■ Season the lamb fillet with salt and pepper. Brown the fillet in the butter and roast in a 175°C oven. Add a drop of water to the roasting tray so the meat does not dry out.

■ Mix the baking powder and salt with the flour. Then add the flour mixture and the puréed potato to the softened butter. Mix the dough until it is smooth and set aside in a cool place for about an hour.

Cut the cabbage and the onion into thin slices and soften in butter. Season with the salt, white pepper and thyme. Press the dough into a buttered pie-dish and spread the cabbage on top. Cook in a 175°C oven for 1–1 1/2 hours. Pour the egg and soured cream mixture over the pie when it has been in the oven for about half an hour.

■ Serve the sliced fillet of lamb with the cabbage pie and roasting juices.

Suitable accompaniments are traditional mutton wines, for example Saint-Emilion or Châteauneuf-du-Pape.

4 SERVINGS

600 G FILLET OF LAMB

SALT AND WHITE PEPPER

1 TBSP BUTTER

WATER

FOR THE CABBAGE PIE:

2 DL FLOUR

1 TSP BAKING POWDER

1 TSP SALT

150 G POTATOES, BOILED AND PURÉED

120 G BUTTER

500 G WHITE CABBAGE

1 ONION

SALT AND PEPPER

THYME

2 DL SOURED CREAM

2 EGGS

600 G PORK FILLET

2 BEETROOTS, UNCOOKED

1 L WATER

SALT

BLACK PEPPER

1 TBSP RED WINE VINEGAR

2 DL SOURED CREAM

PORK FILLET WITH A BEETROOT AND SOURED CREAM SAUCE

■ Wash and peel the beetroots. Boil in slightly salted water until tender. Remove the beetroots from the saucepan and continue to simmer the liquid until it has halved in volume. Add the pepper and the red wine vinegar. Sieve the liquid and add the soured cream, whisking constantly, and finally check the seasoning.

■ Season the fillets with salt and freshly ground black pepper. Brown the fillets in a frying pan and then roast them in the oven.

■ Make a pool of the sauce on each plate. Cut diagonal slices from each fillet and place them on the sauce. Chop the cooked, warm beetroots into small cubes and use them as a garnish. Serve with, for example, steamed green vegetables and a little potato gratin.

Good choices of wine include a white Gewürztraminer from Alsace or a Hungarian Egri Bikavér.

ROAST LAMB IN A WOODEN TROUGH OR *särä*

■ Rub salt into the surface of the joint, put it in a plastic bag, and set aside in a cool place for 48 hours.

Peel the vegetables and chop them into small cubes. Cut up the shallots.

Dry the salted lamb and grind white pepper on to the surface. Place the vegetables and a little water in the bottom of the roasting trough and place the joint on top of them. Add the allspice. Roast at 150°C for about four hours. Some shingles soaked in water should be placed under the *särä* to prevent it burning and splitting.

■ Serve the meat and vegetables straight from the wooden trough.

To drink, a medium full-bodied Bordeaux from the Médoc area would be a good choice. .

4–6 SERVINGS

1 1/2 KG JOINT OF LAMB
2 DL COARSE SALT
3 CARROTS
1 SMALL SWEDE
10 SHALLOTS
A LITTLE WATER FOR THE BASE OF THE *SÄRÄ*
10 ALLSPICE PEPPERCORNS

WOODEN ROASTING TROUGH OR *särä*

4 SERVINGS

100 G HALVA

4 EGG YOLKS

1/2 DL ICING SUGAR

1/2 TSP VANILLA SUGAR

1 TBSP LEMON JUICE

2 DL WHIPPING CREAM

PARFAIT OF HALVA

■ Beat the egg whites and the icing sugar together. Heat in a bain marie until the mixture thickens.

Whisk until cold and add the other ingredients, the whipping cream last. Pour the mixture into a bowl rinsed with cold water and place in the freezer overnight.

Dip the bowl quickly in hot water and turn the parfait out on to a dish.

■ Serve with a berry sauce (see page 80).

STRAWBERRIES IN SPARKLING WINE JELLY

■ Soak the gelatine leaves for 10 minutes in cold water.

Boil the water and sugar and allow to cool. Squeeze the gelatine leaves dry and put them in the syrup to melt. Pour the sparkling wine into the liquid. Mix carefully, so that additional bubbles do not develop in the liquid.

Slice the strawberries, place the slices neatly in a wide champagne glass and pour the lukewarm liquid over them. Let the dessert set, covered, in a cool place for at least 4 hours.

■ Serve with ice-cream or whipped cream.

4 SERVINGS

500 G RIPE STRAWBERRIES

3 LEAVES GELATINE

1 DL WATER

1 DL SUGAR

2 DL SWEET SPARKLING WINE

FOR THE WAFERS:

1 EGG

1/2 DL SUGAR

50 G MELTED BUTTER

1/2 DL WHIPPING CREAM

100 G FLOUR

FOR THE WILD STRAWBERRY CURD CHEESE:

160 G WILD STRAWBERRIES

80 G FROZEN STRAWBERRIES

1 TSP LEMON JUICE

1 1/2 DL SUGAR

250 G CURD CHEESE

1 1/2 DL WHIPPING CREAM

WILD STRAWBERRY CURD CHEESE IN A WAFER SHELL

■ Beat together the eggs and the sugar. Mix in the other ingredients, leaving the flour until last. Shape six thin discs on baking paper, each around 10 cm in diameter. Bake in a hot, 250°C oven for about 3 or 4 minutes, until the wafers have taken on some colour. Remove from the oven and shape into rolls immediately. Keep in a dry place until serving.

■ Purée the strawberries and flavour the purée with the lemon juice and sugar. Reserve a quarter of the purée to make a sauce. Mix the curd cheese with the whipped cream and then add the strawberry purée.

■ Fill the wafer rolls with curd cheese and serve with the sauce.

APPLE AND CINNAMON SORBETS

■ Begin by mixing all the ingredients of the cinnamon sorbet except the egg white and simmer the mixture on a medium heat for one hour. Cool the mixture and add the stiffly beaten egg white. Turn the mixture into a sorbet using an ice-cream making machine and put it in the freezer.

■ Mix the apple cubes, sugar and water. Simmer the mixture until the apple cubes are soft. Purée. Add the remaining ingredients to the cooled mixture and mix to a sorbet in an ice-cream maker.

■ Bring the cream and the cinnamon stick to the boil. Beat the eggs and sugar lightly and whisk the mixture into the hot cream. Continue to cook in a bain marie, whisking constantly, until the sauce thickens.

■ Whisk the sauce until cold and, finally, remove the cinnamon stick.

■ Place the apple sorbet in small ring moulds. Remove the apple mould and place a thin almond biscuit on top of the sorbet.

■ Place some cinnamon sorbet on top of the apple sorbet with a spoon and serve with cinnamon sauce and berry sauce (see page 80).

10 SERVINGS

FOR THE CINNAMON SORBET:

7 DL MILK
2 CINNAMON STICKS
1 1/2 DL SUGAR
1 TSP OLIVE OIL
1 EGG WHITE

FOR THE APPLE SORBET:

500 G APPLES, CUT INTO SMALL CUBES
200 G SUGAR
3 DL WATER
1 TBSP LEMON JUICE
1 EGG WHITE, BEATEN
1/2 DL CALVADOS OR VODKA

FOR THE CINNAMON SAUCE:

3 DL SINGLE CREAM
1 CINNAMON STICK
4–5 EGG YOLKS
80 G SUGAR

NIGHT OF

A THOUSAND

PINCERS

It begins as the evening darkens, and every year on the same day, 21 July. By the afternoon hours, the first pincer-wielders have been tempted out of their lairs. Then they have swum again in a large saucepan with sprigs of crown dill, and exchanged their original brown-grey colour for a positively sinful scarlet. Having cooled slowly in their cooking liquid through the early evening, they now wait, in a large bowl, for the beginning of their first-night ceremonies.

The rituals of the crayfish dinner follow a long and tested tradition. A table is

crayfish. It is slightly broader in girl crayfish than in boy crayfish. So the expert keeps an eye on the girls, and lets the more inexperienced guests pick out the boys, with their larger pincers.

To accompany the pincers, the crayfish table is laid with sufficient quantities of toast, chopped dill and schnapps. The peeled and cleaned tail is placed carefully on buttered toast and covered neatly with chopped dill.

By now the evening's host has taken good care that each guest's small, frost-covered glass is full of the hard stuff, for example Finnish vodka. (For good schnapps recipes turn to pages 31–33). Everyone now tucks into their first tail and raises their glass, with the classic toast: *kippis*!

laid outdoors, weather (even remotely) permitting. And because a rather messy struggle for the delicacies beneath the red armour is anticipated, each diner wears a generously sized crayfish bib of cloth or paper around his neck and a bunch of paper napkins on his lap and beside his plate. In his hands he has a small but efficient crayfish knife.

In outdoor and indoor markets, crayfish are sold individually either living or cooked, when they gain their bright red colour. So, when planning a crayfish dinner, a suitable number is generally reserved for each guest. Ten is generally considered a good number when the crayfish are to be enjoyed as, for example, a starter. A real aficionado can get through twenty without difficulty, and will happily leave the main course to the other guests.

Cooking crayfish is a simple but very delicate art-form. In addition to water and coarse salt, a good bunch of fresh crown dill is necessary, and, preferably, a lump or two of sugar, depending on the quantity of the crustaceans. The rest is almost occultism. Some add beer to the liquid, some a drop of wine vinegar or a couple of cloves of garlic. A perfect result, nevertheless, always demands years of practice. So perfect recipes are seldom made public or even confided to friends.

Eating begins with sucking all the noble aromas of the successful cooking liquid from the surface of the crayfish. Then it is the turn of the crustacean's moving parts. The pincers are split open and the flesh is dug out using the crayfish knife. The tail is detached from the back-armour, from which all possible crayfish butter is carefully scraped.

In the culinary sense, the tail is the most important part of the

The ceremony is repeated each time a new tail takes its turn. Instead of schnapps, beer or mineral water, many people now also drink wine at crayfish dinners. It is entirely in accordance with etiquette, and does not prevent one from participating in the cheerful, multilingual and polyphonic sch-

napps songs that may be sung by the dozen as the night wears on.

The main course of a crayfish dinner is often small and light, for example smoked fish or the first fried chanterelles of the season. Dessert might consist of fresh raspberries, strawberries or black- or redcurrants.

It is not entirely necessary to throw empty crayfish shells away. If you have the energy, you can make a stock of them the next day, which can then form the base for an excellent soup or sauce.

AUTUMN

AT FIRST, THE COMING OF AUTUMN IS HARDLY NOTICEABLE

The first signs of autumn can, it is true, be sensed early on – in fact, they are already present when summer feels at its height. The chanterelle mushrooms that appear at the end of July are the first reminder, for Finns, of the inevitable approach of the long,

dark autumn. In spite of that, they are happy to carry the harvest they have gathered themselves into the kitchen of their summer house and enjoy mushrooms as they are, fried in butter or stewed in cream.

Hundreds of edible mushrooms grow in the Finnish forests. A total of around thirty varieties are worth picking, of which ten qualify as commercial mushrooms. In addition to chanterelles, they include, for example, ceps, milk caps, horns-of-

Photo: Paavo Merikukka/LKA

Photo: Pauli Nieminen/LKA

Finns have also learned to make excellent liqueurs from their berries. Of them, cloudberry liqueur is probably the most widely known abroad, but it faces tough competition from a liqueur distilled from the rare arctic bramble, which was once one of the favourite drinks of the court at St Petersburg.

SHOOT-OUTS IN THE RUSHES

The twentieth of August marks the beginning of busy times for wild ducks. Their rush-beds are filled with splashing and banging, and gunpowder smoke hangs thickly in the air. Many a duck ends up as a roast with sweet sauerkraut or sea buckthorn berry sauce.

The wild duck is one of those game birds that one can only taste at a restaurant table or at the dinner table of a huntsman friend. Such invitations should be accepted without hesitation, since they are rarely forthcoming.

Photo: Asko Hämäläinen/LKA

plenty and funnel-shaped chanterelles. All of them can be used, after cleaning, in cooking without further preparation – fried or boiled for freezing, or preserved in brine or vinegar.

JAM IS NOT THE ONLY USE
FOR AUTUMN BERRIES

In the good old days, late summer and early autumn were a golden age of the sugar industry. In almost every kitchen an imposing saucepan simmered day after day, turning autumn berries into syrup and jam. The preserving season began with the first strawberries of the summer and ended only when the last lingonberries and cloudberries have been safely packed away in glass jars and hidden away in the cellar. Jams and syrups are still made today, but the freezer has superseded the preserving pan.

THOSE MAGNIFICENT MEN
IN THEIR RED CAPS

Anyone who participates in a moose hunt must wear a red cap and a red coat or waistcoat. The intention is not to frighten the life out of the moose, but to allow the hunters to see each other. At the beginning of the moose-hunting season, these red caps are to be seen in the autumn countryside in their hundreds.

The moose is Finland's most coveted game animal, and its hunting is subject to licence. In recent years, approximately 50,000 hunting licences have been granted annually. In the best hunting seasons, so many animals are shot that there is enough meat for some to make its way into the shops and the saucepans of ordinary consumers. Moose meat is, of course, more expensive than beef,

but cheaper parts of game carcasses are used enthusiastically in various casserole dishes.

Good supplies of moose flesh have inspired cooks to experiment with new and interesting recipes. Dishes made with raw steak have become popular, such as *carpaccio*, made in the Italian style, *riimi* (marinated) and fresh-salted.

AT THE BALTIC HERRING MARKETS

The autumnal Baltic herring market bring dozens of fishing boats to Helsinki's central market from up and down the shores of the Gulf of Finland, some of them from great distances. Among them always are visitors from as far away as the Åland islands.

The fishing boats tethered at the jetties and the stalls set up on dry land are bursting with Baltic herring in all its possible forms. There is fresh herring, smoked herring, spicy herring preserved in little wooden barrels, poor man's salmon, herring in mustard sauce, fried herring fillets in vinegar sauce, cooked rollmop her-

rings... On market days, the city's restaurants, too, vie with each other for the best herring dish of the year.

In the autumn fish market or covered market you may also encounter a fish far stranger than the Baltic herring. Somehow it recalls a small eel — but it is no eel, but the lamprey, which lives in the rivers of the west coast.

Lampreys are sold grilled or roasted, marinaded in a vinegar sauce. A grilled lamprey tastes best as it is, with a strong mustard sauce. For some unknown reason, the lamprey is now also generally known as the 'liquor worm'.

A PIECE OF OUR DAILY BREAD

The respect Finns feel for bread has as its background the hard lessons of past centuries. Frost was a frequent visitor to the infertile farmlands of the north and even the south, and a flour milled from pine bark was universally used to make grain go further. The last great famine years were experienced in 1867–68.

In these northerly latitudes, the farming of grain for bread has always demanded an optimistic spirit and a great deal of hard work. In the minds of contemporary Finnish farmers, however, as they struggle with problems of over-production and marketing, frost and famine are probably no longer prime worries.

D ark rye bread or sour-dough bread – whatever we choose to call it – isthe basic type of Finnish bread. It has been baked and eaten for centuries in both eastern and western Finland. Similar doughs, however, were made into different breads. In eastern Finland, the oven was known at an early date, and it was used on a daily basis in the preparation of food. Thus bread, too, was baked often, and eaten fresh. In western Finland, baking generally took place only a couple of times a year, and the loaves were preserved by drying them on poles hung from the ceiling of the cottage. It is for this reason that eastern Finnish rye loaves are round and soft, while the western Finnish version is flat and hard, with a hole in the middle.

Among the almost rock-hard western Finnish hole-bread's relatives, the various crisp, dried sour-dough breads are popular, as is the half-hard *jälkiuunileipä* (bread baked at low temperatures for a very long time) and the crispbreads that have been adapted from our western neighbour. Western influences are also evident in many of the sweet breads that will be familiar to anyone who has travelled in the southern and south-western archipelagos.

THE SECRET OF SOUR-DOUGH BREAD IS IN THE LEAVEN

In the olden days, every house had a large wooden bowl that was used only for making sour-dough. And it was never washed. The secret is that the old dough that is left around the edges of the bowl acts, like yeast, as a raising and souring agent for the new dough. Such dough-tubs are still in use in some country houses, and the leaven they contain is often known to have been used by bakers over several generations.

Today's home bread-maker saves a small piece of the dough as the leaven for the next dough. It keeps well in the freezer, until it is needed once more. If no root is available, the dough can be soured by soaking small pieces of rye bread or sour-dough rusks,

or rye flour mixed with yeast, in lukewarm boiled water. The leaven is ready after the mixture has been allowed to sour at room temperature for 24–48 hours.

NO OVEN WAS NEEDED TO MAKE *rieska*

Rieska is a flat bread made from unleavened dough that is baked quickly in a hot oven or on stones and eaten immediately. Because *rieska* can be made without an oven, it was a very common bread in western Finland and Lapland from ancient times.

But there are also *rieska*s that have long been baked in the ovens of the eastern Finns. *Rieska* dough is made from water, milk or buttermilk, and flour. The commonest flours are barley and buckwheat; potato flour can be used in addition.

THE PASTY THAT BECAME A NATIONAL INSTITUTION

The Karelian pasty is much more than rice pudding baked in a paper-thin rye-dough shell. It has, in a way, become the symbol of the entire Karelian culture and a memento of the old Finnish province, which no longer exists as older Finns still remember it.

Although the pasty has, along with Karelian migrants, found its path on to nearly every Finnish coffee and festive table, the real masters of its making are a disappearing natural resource.

The baking of Karelian pasties is an art. For how else could one explain the fact that rice or barley porridge or mashed potato in a shell made of water and rye flour can, at its best, take one's tongue with it – even without the egg-butter mixture that is usually spread on top?

THE KARELIAN PASTY AND THE FISH PASTY COME FROM A GREAT FAMILY

Many of the relatives of the Karelian pasty are also known on the other side of the border, in Russia.

The mother of the *kalakukko* of Savo is called the *kurniekka*, chicken baked in a wheat- or rye-flour case. From this typically Russian pie it is only a short step to the *kalakukko*, or fish pasty, which is filled not with one big fish but with many small ones, perch or vendace.

A salmon pasty enclosed in a puff pastry case, the *kulibiaka*, belongs, of course, among the nobility of Russian-born pasties: it is also known as one of the classics of French cuisine.

FINNISH SOUR-DOUGH BREAD

■ Make the first dough by mixing 2 dl of old dough root with 1 l lukewarm water. Instead, you can use 1–2 powdered sour-dough rusks or slices of rye bread or 20 g yeast. Add 500 g rye flour to the dough and allow it to sour at room temperature for 24–48 hours, until it bubbles and tastes sour. Add 2 tbsp salt and 500–700 g rye flour to the dough. Knead it on a table sprinkled with rye flour or in a food processor. Reserve a piece of the dough for the next baking and make the rest of the dough into two round loaves, or divide it among a number of bread moulds. Allow the loaves to rise under a cloth until they have doubled in size and prick them. Bake in a 230°C oven for 1–1 1/2 hours. The loaves are ready when they boom when tapped on the base. Cover the cooked loaves with a cloth and allow to cool before serving.

UNLEAVENED BARLEY BREAD

1 L BUTTERMILK OR MILK
2 TSP SALT
1 TSP SODA, IF YOU ARE USING
BUTTERMILK AS THE LIQUID
2 DL WHEAT FLOUR
1 KG BARLEY FLOUR

■ Dissolve the salt in the buttermilk. Mix the soda with both types of flour and knead to a thickish dough. Make the dough into flattish cakes, prick them with a fork and bake until ready in a 250°C oven.

MALT LOAF

1 L BUTTERMILK
2 PIECES OF YEAST
3 DL MALT
3 DL WHOLEWHEAT FLOUR
3 DL WHEAT BRAN
10–13 DL FLOUR
1 TBSP SALT
3 DL SYRUP

■ Warm the buttermilk to room temperature and dissolve the yeast in it. Rub the malt lightly. Combine all ingredients and let the dough rise for about one and a half hours. The dough can be fairly soft. Divide the dough among three bread moulds and bake in a 175°C oven for 1 1/2 hours. Brush the loaves with the syrup when they have been in the oven for an hour.

SALMON KULIBIAKA

4 SERVINGS

300 G SALMON FILLET, SLICED

1 DL WHOLE BARLEY GRAINS

WATER, SALT

1 LARGE ONION

100 G BUTTER

WHITE PEPPER, GROUND

400 G PUFF PASTRY

4 TBSP DILL, CHOPPED

3 HARD-BOILED EGGS

EGG FOR GLAZING

■ Simmer the barley grains in salted water until they are tender (about 20 minutes). Sieve the barley and rinse it in cold water; drain. Chop the onion and soften it in a frying pan in 1 tbsp of the butter. Melt the rest of the butter and pour it into the barley. Season with salt and pepper. Set the mixture aside in a cool place. Roll out the puff pastry to a 35 x 35 cm rectangle.

Place half of the barley on the pastry, leaving an 8 cm border to the right, 15 cm to the left, and 4 cm at either end. On top of the barley place layers of onion, dill, sliced salmon; top with slices of hard-boiled egg and, finally, the rest of the barley. Season each layer with salt and ground pepper.

Glaze the edges of the pasty with egg and turn first the ends, then the right side, and finally the left, of the pastry over on to the filling. Make sure the seams are firmly secured. Garnish the pasty and glaze with egg. Prick the case with a fork.

Bake the pasty at 225°C for the first 15 minutes, and then, for 30–40 minutes, at 180–200°C. If the pasty darkens too much in the final stages of cooking, cover it with aluminium foil.

■ Serve with melted butter and soured cream.

STARTERS

500 G FILLET OF MOOSE

1 TBSP SEA SALT

1 TSP CRUSHED PEPPERS

4 SPRIGS OF FRESH THYME

5 CRUSHED JUNIPER BERRIES

2 CL GIN

FOR THE MARINATED MUSHROOMS:

500 G CEPS OR

CHANTERELLES

1 ONION

1 SMALL CARROT

FOR THE STOCK:

1/2 DL LIQUOR VINEGAR

100 G SUGAR

3 DL WATER

CLOVES

6 WHITE PEPPERS

1 BAY LEAF

1 TSP SALT

FRESH-SALTED MOOSE STEAK WITH MACERATED MUSHROOMS

■ Remove all membranes from the fillet and place it on a piece of kitchen film. Rub the salt and spices into the surface. Add the gin. Wrap the fillet tightly in the kitchen film and macerate in the refrigerator for 48 hours. Turn the bag from time to time so that the meat macerates evenly.

■ Chop the cleaned mushrooms and slice the onion and carrot.

■ Bring the stock to the boil. Place the vegetables in layers in a glass jar and pour the stock over. Marinate for at least 48 hours.

■ Before serving, place the meat in the freezer for a moment.

■ Cut thin slices from the cold fillet with a very sharp knife. Serve with the marinated mushrooms. (If you wish, you can also freeze the meat for later use.)

REINDEER TONGUE MOUSSE
WITH CRANBERRY-HORSERADISH SAUCE

■ Mince the cleaned and peeled tongues in a food processor with the game sauce. Add the lukewarm meat stock, in which you have dissolved the gelatine leaves, and mix. Finally, add the whipped cream. Pour the mixture into a bowl and cover with kitchen film

■ Crush the cranberries lightly and mix in the sugar. Add the orange juice and mustard. Press the jelly through a sieve and mix in the port. Mix both parts together and, finally, add the grated horseradish.

■ Using a spoon dipped in warm water, form the congealed reindeer tongues into egg-shapes.

■ Serve with cranberry-horseradish sauce and decorate with cranberries.

6—8 SERVINGS

500 G SMOKED REINDEER	
TONGUES, BOILED	
2 DL GAME SAUCE	
1 1/2 DL MEAT STOCK	
2 GELATINE LEAVES, SOAKED	
2 DL WHIPPING CREAM	

FOR THE CRANBERRY-HORSERADISH SAUCE:

75 G CRANBERRIES	
1/2 DL SUGAR	
JUICE OF 1 ORANGE	
1 TSP FRENCH MUSTARD	
125 G CRANBERRY JELLY	
1/2 DL PORT	
1/2 DL HORSERADISH, GRATED	

4 SERVINGS

500 G BALTIC HERRING FILLETS

2 TBSP WHITE WINE VINEGAR

2 DL WATER

1 SMALL ONION

2 TBSP DILL, CHOPPED

1 TBSP DIJON MUSTARD

1 TBSP LEMON JUICE

COARSELY GROUND WHITE PEPPER

SALT

4 SLICES RYE BREAD

BUTTER

4 TSP ROE TO GARNISH

BALTIC HERRING TARTARE

■ Remove the skin from the Baltic herring fillets. Mix the vinegar and water, pour it over the herrings and marinate them in the refrigerator for about half an hour.

Drain the herring fillets carefully in a sieve. Cut 400 g of the fillets crossways into thin slices; leave the remainder whole.

Chop the onion and the dill and mix into the herrings. Season with mustard and lemon juice. Add the coarsely ground white pepper, and salt according to taste. Mix thoroughly.

■ Cut the slices of bread using a ring mould and butter them. Set the mould on the bread. Line the inner surface of the mould with herring fillets and pack the mould tightly with the herring mixture. Remove the mould and garnish the tartare with a teaspoonful of vendace or rainbow trout roe.

FRESH-SALTED SALMON WITH WARM BEETROOT SALAD

■ Place the salmon fillet on a piece of baking paper, skin side down. Mix the white pepper, sugar and salt. Sprinkle the mixture evenly on the surface of the salmon. Place the sprigs of dill on top and wrap the salmon tightly in baking paper. Put the salmon in a cold place and macerate for 24 hours.

■ Cut the beetroot into fingertip-sized cubes and chop the onion. Soften the onion in butter on a low heat. Add the beetroot and the grated horseradish. Season with salt and white pepper. Add the soured cream and bring the salad to the boil.

■ Take the salmon out of the cold, remove the spices from its surface and cut into thin slices. Serve with the beetroot salad.

Suitable wines would include a fresh, acidic Sancerre or a Sauvignon Blanc from the New World.

8 SERVINGS

1 KG BONELESS FILLET OF

SEA SALMON

1 TSP COARSELY GROUND

WHITE PEPPER

2 TSP SUGAR

2 TSP COARSE SALT

SPRIGS OF DILL

FOR THE BEETROOT SALAD:

BEETROOT COOKED IN

VINEGAR

1 ONION

1 TSP BUTTER

1 TSP GRATED HORSERADISH

SALT

GROUND WHITE PEPPER

2 TSP SOURED CREAM

6 SERVINGS

| 12 RIVER CRAYFISH, BOILED |
| 3 TBSP BUTTER |
| 1 ONION |
| 2 TBSP TOMATO PURÉE |
| 7 DL DRY WHITE WINE |
| 7 DL FISH STOCK |
| 1 TSP DRIED THYME |
| 1/4 TSP CAYENNE PEPPER |
| 1 TBSP FLOUR |
| SALT |
| 2 DL CREAM |

RIVER CRAYFISH SOUP

■ Peel the crayfish and reserve the tail and pincer flesh. Crush the shells thoroughly. Melt the butter in a saucepan and fry the crayfish shells on a low heat. Add the chopped onion and the tomato purée. Continue to cook for a moment.

Pour the white wine and the fish stock into the pan. Cook on a low heat for one hour. If you simmer too long at too high a temperature, the soup will taste of ammonia. Season the stock with thyme and cayenne pepper and continue to simmer for about half an hour. Sieve the liquid through muslin, squeezing all the stock from the crayfish shells. Put the stock aside in a cold place overnight.

Remove the crayfish butter that has gathered on the surface of the stock and melt it in a saucepan. Add the flour and cook for a moment on a low heat. Add the stock and boil, uncovered, until one third of the stock has evaporated.

■ Season the soup with salt and mix in the whipped cream and the tail and pincer flesh.

JERUSALEM ARTICHOKE SOUP
WITH HORNS OF PLENTY

■ Peel the Jerusalem artichokes, cut them into fingertip-sized cubes and place in the milk. Set aside.

Cut the pale part of the leek into strips and chop the onion finely. Melt the butter in a saucepan and add the Jerusalem artichokes, the onion and the leek; simmer — do not brown — for a few minutes. Add the flour. When it is fully absorbed, add the stock in two or three batches, stirring thoroughly.

Simmer gently, partially covered, for about 30 minutes. Purée the soup in a liquidiser, sieve if necessary and season with salt and pepper. Lastly, add the cream, which you have brought to the boil.

■ Ladle the soup into bowls and garnish each with a couple of crushed horns of plenty.

4 SERVINGS

500 G JERUSALEM ARTICHOKES

2 DL MILK

THE PALE PART OF HALF A LEEK

HALF A MEDIUM-SIZED ONION

60 G BUTTER

30 G FLOUR

1 L LIGHT MEAT STOCK

SALT AND PEPPER

2 DL CREAM

2 DRIED HORN-OF-PLENTY MUSHROOMS PER PORTION

4 SERVINGS	FOR THE SMOKED RAINBOW TROUT ROE SAUCE:
2 PIKE-PERCH FILLETS OF 200 G	1/2 DL WHITE WINE VINEGAR
4 SLICES OF SALMON OF 200 G	1/2 DL WATER
SALT AND WHITE PEPPER	1 DL WHITE WINE
20 G BUTTER	2 SHALLOTS, FINELY CHOPPED
WATER	100 G UNSALTED BUTTER
	1 TSP LEMON JUICE
	GROUND WHITE PEPPER
	120 G SMOKED RAINBOW
	TROUT ROE

PIKE-PERCH—SALMON MEDALLIONS WITH ROE SAUCE

■ Cut the pike-perch fillets in half lengthways and season with salt and white pepper. Place the salmon slices on top and form into a roll.

Butter four ring moulds and an ovenproof dish. Place the fish rolls in the ring moulds and salt and pepper them lightly. Place the ring moulds in the ovenproof dish, pour a little water into the base of the dish and cover with aluminium foil. Bake in a 200°C oven for about 10 minutes.

■ Place the wine vinegar, water, wine and chopped shallot in a sauce pan. Simmer until the mixture is reduced to a quarter of its original volume

Take the pan from the heat and whisk in the chopped, cold butter. Heat and season with lemon and white pepper. Sieve the sauce and add the smoked rainbow trout roe. Keep the sauce warm but do not allow to boil.

■ Make a pool of the sauce on each plate. Remove the ring moulds and place the rolls on the sauce-pool.

A good choice of wine would be a dry and acidic Pouilly-Fuissé or a Chablis.

BALTIC HERRING PATTIES

■ Place half the herring fillets on baking paper, skin side down. Season with salt and pepper, and sprinkle with the chopped dill or chives. Cover with the remaining herring fillets, skin side up. Roll the patties in rye flour. Fry the patties in butter until golden-brown on both sides. Serve at once.

■ A good accompaniment for Baltic herring patties is, for example, mashed potatoes mixed with a little chopped, braised leek.

To drink, the best choice is beer or mineral water.

4 SERVINGS

32 BALTIC HERRING FILLETS

SALT AND WHITE PEPPER

DILL OR CHIVES, CHOPPED

RYE FLOUR

BUTTER FOR FRYING

4 SERVINGS

4 130 G PIECES FILLET OF

LAMB, COMPLETELY CLEANED

120 G LONG, THIN SLICES OF

BACON

2 TBSP BUTTER

15 G CARROTS, CUT INTO

SMALL CUBES

15 G CELERIAC, CUT INTO

SMALL CUBES

15 G ONION, FINELY CHOPPED

15 G SWEDE OR TURNIP,

CUT INTO SMALL CUBES

HALF A GARLIC CLOVE

40 FRESH MUSHROOMS

2 TBSP PARSLEY, FINELY

CHOPPED

SALT AND PEPPER

**FOR THE COURGETTE
GRATIN:**

500 G COURGETTES

WATER AND SEA SALT

2 DL WHIPPING CREAM

A LITTLE SALT AND COARSELY

GROUND BLACK PEPPER

80 G COARSELY GRATED

BLUE CHEESE

1/2 TBSP BUTTER

LAMB STEAKS WRAPPED IN BACON

■ Melt a tablespoonful of butter in a saucepan and stew the cubed vegetables, sliced garlic and mushrooms on a low heat, covered, until they are soft. Finally, add the parsley, season with salt and pepper and allow to cool.

■ Brown the lamb fillets in butter on a medium heat. Season with salt and pepper and allow to cool. The fillets should be completely raw at the centre. Make pockets lengthways in the fillet pieces. Fill them with the vegetable mixture and wrap the bacon slices tightly around them. Place the bundles in a buttered oven dish.

■ Split the washed courgettes and cut them into 1/2 cm slices. Blanch them in rapidly boiling water seasoned with sea salt for 1 minute. Pour into a sieve, shake the water off and return to the pan with the heated cream. Cook for 3 minutes and remove the pan from the heat. Season with salt and black pepper and mix in the grated blue cheese. Butter a low oven dish. Add the courgette mixture and place under the grill until the surface is nut-brown.

■ Heat the oven to 250°C and bake the lamb fillets for 6–8 minutes. Place the fillets in a dish and keep them warm under a piece of aluminium foil for about 10 minutes before serving.

A red wine sauce (page 21) makes a good accompaniment for this dish.

To drink, try a red wine from the Penedés region or an Australian Shiraz.

REINDEER FILLET BAKED IN UNLEAVENED POTATO BREAD

■ Season the reindeer fillet with salt and finely ground white pepper. Cut the fillet into four equal-sized pieces and brown them in butter in a hot pan. Let the fillets cool.

■ Mix the egg and buttermilk into the puréed potatoes. Combine all the dry ingredients and add to the potato mixture. Knead the dough lightly and roll out on a floured surface to a thickness of 1/2 cm. Carefully dust the flour off the surface of the dough.

Place the fillet pieces on the dough and roll the dough around them. Sprinkle the edges and seams with water to ensure that the parcels stay closed. Glaze the parcels with buttermilk and prick the surface with a fork to prevent the dough from tearing during baking. Bake at 225°C for 10–15 minutes.

■ Serve with game sauce and steamed vegetables.

A good accompaniment would be a Médoc or a Cabernet Sauvignon from the New World.

4 SERVINGS

600 G REINDEER FILLET, CLEANED

SALT AND WHITE PEPPER

1 TBSP BUTTER

FOR THE UNLEAVENED POTATO BREAD DOUGH:

300 G POTATOES, BOILED AND PURÉED

1 EGG

1 DL BUTTERMILK

1 TSP SODA

1 DL RYE FLOUR

2 1/2 DL WHEAT FLOUR

1 TSP SALT

FOR THE JUNIPER-BERRY SAUCE:

500 G REINDEER STEAK

8 PIECES OF BACON

SALT AND PEPPER

3 DL DARK BASIC SAUCE

2 DL RED WINE

10 JUNIPER BERRIES, CRUSHED

FOR THE STUFFING:

1 SMALL ONION, FINELY CHOPPED

1 TBSP BUTTER

100 G CHANTERELLE MUSHROOMS, FINELY CHOPPED

100 G FRESH SPINACH

SALT AND FRESHLY GROUND WHITE PEPPER

FOR THE MUSHROOM-POTATO TIMBALE:

2 POTATOES

100 G MIXED MUSHROOMS

1/2 ONION

50 G BUTTER

SALT AND WHITE PEPPER

1 DL SOURED CREAM

REINDEER STEAK STUFFED WITH SPINACH AND CHANTERELLES

■ Cut the reindeer steak almost in half lengthways so that it opens like a book. Then pound the meat lightly between two layers plastic film.

■ Soften the onion in butter. Add the chanterelles and the blanched spinach, simmer and season. Allow to cool. Spread the filling evenly over the opened steak and roll the steak up to form a roulade. Wrap the bacon around the roulade. Brown the fillet in a hot pan and season. Bake for about six minutes in a 180°C oven; the meat should remain a handsome pink colour inside.

■ Mix the sauce ingredients together and boil until reduced to a third in volume. Sieve the sauce and keep warm.

■ Peel and slice the potatoes. Place them in alternate layers with the mushroom-onion mixture and then add the soured cream. Bake in a 180°C oven for about half an hour.

■ Serve the sauce on to plates. Cut the cooked steak into slices and place on the pools of sauce. Serve with the mushroom-potato timbale.

    Suitable wines include a mature Saint-Emilion or a Tuscan Brunello di Montalcino.

MOOSE TOURNEDOS
WITH DARK SAUERKRAUT

■ One day in advance: Remove the membranes from the well-hung fillet of moose (use the central part of the fillet, if possible). Mix the marinade and place the meat, in a plastic bag, in a cold place to macerate for 24 hours.

Make a game stock from the moose bones and scraps and the root vegetables. Simmer the stock until it is reduced to about 1/2 l.

■ Rinse the sauerkraut and put it in a pan with the diced bacon and glaze well. Add the wine, the dark game stock, the water and seasonings. Simmer in the pot for a couple of hours.

■ Cut the fillet into four large pieces. Wrap the slices of lard around the pieces of fillet and secure them with thread. Fry the tournedos in butter until they are medium rare.

■ Place the sauerkraut on plates and set the tournedos on top of the sauerkraut.

A good choice of wine would be, for example, a full-bodied Côtes du Rhône or a Spanish red from the Penedés area.

4 SERVINGS

700 G FILLET OF MOOSE

160 G FINELY SLICED LARD

OR SPECK

SALT AND WHITE PEPPER

BUTTER FOR FRYING

FOR THE MARINADE:

1/2 DL OIL

1/2 DL BALSAMIC VINEGAR

2 SPRIGS THYME

1 BAY LEAF

A LITTLE COARSELY GROUND

WHITE PEPPER

**FOR THE DARK
SAUERKRAUT:**

500 G SAUERKRAUT

100 G BACON

1 DL RED WINE

5 DL GAME STOCK,

MADE FROM BONES AND

ROOT VEGETABLES

2 DL WATER

20 CARAWAY SEEDS

6 JUNIPER BERRIES

WILD DUCK IN A SEA BUCKTHORN SAUCE

4 SERVINGS	FOR THE BUCKTHORN SAUCE:
2 WILD DUCKS	1/2 DL SUGAR
SALT AND WHITE PEPPER	1/2 DL BUCKTHORN JUICE
1 CARROT	1 DL COOKING JUICES FROM
1 ONION	THE WILD DUCKS
A PIECE OF CELERIAC	2 DL CREAM
2 DL WATER	

■ If sea buckthorn juice is not available we suggest a juice obtained by macerating dried apricots overnight in water. Rinse the prepared ducks, dry them and rub the seasonings into the skin. Truss the birds. Dice the carrots, the small onion and the celeriac. Place in the bottom of a roasting tray with the birds' wings and necks. Place the ducks on top, breast sides up.

Pour about 2 dl water into the tray. Roast in a 180°C oven for 50 minutes. Take the ducks from the roasting tray and keep them warm. Boil the cooking juices for another 15 minutes.

■ Heat the sugar until it colours and add the buckthorn juice; bring to the boil. Add the sieved duck cooking juices and, after a moment, the cream, and simmer until thickened.

■ Bone the ducks, place the meat on plates and pour the hot sauce beside them. Serve with, for example, noodles garnished with lingonberries.

A Cabernet Sauvignon from the Napa Valley, California is a good choice for the wine.

WILLOW GROUSE
WITH REDCURRANT SAUCE AND BEETROOT

■ Remove the breasts from the grouse and make a stock from the carcasses. Put the stock and the redcurrants in a saucepan and reduce by one third. Sieve the stock and thicken it with the arrowroot. Season the sauce with the salt and ground white pepper.

■ Cut the black salsify into 1/2 cm pieces and cook in butter for 5 minutes. Sprinkle with the flour and mix thoroughly. Add the cream and the soured cream. Cook on a medium heat for 10 minutes, stirring occasionally. Finally, season with salt and white pepper.

■ Season the grouse breasts with salt and ground white pepper. Brown the breasts well on both sides and then cook in a 175°C oven for about 5 minutes. Allow the breasts to stand, covered with a cloth, for 5 minutes.

■ Serve the breasts with black salsify and redcurrant sauce.

   Suitable wines include Burgundy from the Côte de Beaune region or a Californian Merlot.

4 SERVINGS

4 WILLOW GROUSE
1 TBSP BUTTER FOR FRYING
4 DL WILLOW GROUSE STOCK
1 DL REDCURRANTS
1 TSP ARROWROOT
WATER
SALT AND GROUND WHITE PEPPER
400 G BLACK SALSIFY, PEELED
2 TBSP BUTTER
1 TBSP FLOUR
1 DL CREAM
1/2 DL SOURED CREAM

4 SERVINGS

2 OVEN-READY WILD DUCK

1 CARROT

1 PARSNIP

A PIECE OF CELERIAC

A PIECE OF LEEK

2 TBSP BUTTER

1 TSP SALT

WHITE PEPPER

500 G SAUERKRAUT

1 ONION

1 APPLE

1 DL TREACLE

3 DL BEER

WILD DUCK WITH SWEET SAUERKRAUT

■ Remove the breast and thigh meat from the duck. Make a stock from the duck carcasses and the vegetables.

Brown the breast and thigh meat in butter in a hot pan and season with salt and ground white pepper.

■ Rinse the sauerkraut in cold water and drain. Chop the onion finely and soften it in butter. Peel and core the apple and cut into small dice.

■ Add the sauerkraut and the apples to the onion. Season with salt and white pepper.

Then add the treacle, beer and duck stock so that the cabbage is well-covered. Simmer, uncovered, until all the liquid has evaporated.

Spread half the sauerkraut on the base of a buttered oven dish with a lid and place the browned duck breast and thigh meat on the sauerkraut. Spread the other half of the sauerkraut over the meat and bake, covered, in a 200°C oven for about an hour. Instead of a lid, you can also cover the dish with a pastry top.

■ Serve with, for example, small onions stewed in cream.

An excellent wine would be a red Côtes du Rhône or a Californian Zinfandel.

PHEASANT WITH DILL

■ Remove the breast and thigh meat from the pheasant and cut them into 2 cm pieces.

Chop the pheasant carcass and the vegetables into approximately 3 cm pieces. Melt the butter in a saucepan and stew the pheasant and vegetable pieces on a medium heat, without browning, for about 10 minutes. Add the flour, meat stock, pepper and bay leaves and cook, covered, on a medium heat for one hour. Sieve the sauce into a separate saucepan and season with salt.

Add the pheasant meat to the sauce and continue to cook for half an hour. Season the sauce with sugar and lemon juice. Bring to the boil again and add the chopped dill.

■ Serve with root vegetables and boiled potatoes.

To drink, a light beer or mineral water would be a good choice.

2 SERVINGS

1 PHEASANT (ABOUT 750 G)

100 G CARROTS, PEELED

50 G CELERIAC, PEELED

150 G LEEKS

50 G PARSNIPS, PEELED

2 TBSP BUTTER

3 TBSP FLOUR

1 L LIGHT MEAT STOCK

15 WHOLE BLACK PEPPERS

2 BAY LEAVES

SALT

1 TSP SUGAR

3 TBSP LEMON JUICE

3 TBSP DILL, CHOPPED

6 SERVINGS

FOR THE SWISS ROLL:

3 EGGS

1 1/2 DL SUGAR

1 TSP BAKING POWDER

3/4 DL POTATO FLOUR

ABOUT 1 DL APPLE SAUCE

FOR THE FILLING:

2 LEAVES GELATINE, WATER

1 EGG

3/4 DL SUGAR

2 DL MILK

2 DL APPLE, FINELY DICED

2 1/2 DL WHIPPED CREAM

FOR THE STRAWBERRY SAUCE:

200 G FROZEN STRAWBERRIES

1/2 DL CITRUS LIQUEUR

1/2 DL SUGAR

APPLE CHARLOTTE

■ Whisk the eggs and sugar until foamy. Mix the baking powder with the potato flour and add to the egg, mixing carefully.

Spread the mixture on to a baking tray lined with baking paper and bake at 200°C for about 10 minutes.

Spread the cooked sponge thinly with apple sauce and roll tightly. Put the roll into the freezer for at least an hour.

■ Soak the gelatine in a generous amount of cold water for 20 minutes.

Whisk the eggs and sugar to a light foam. Mix the foam with the heated milk and cook the mixture in a bain marie for about 10 minutes, until it has thickened. Remove the mixture from the bain marie and whisk until cool.

Squeeze the gelatine leaves dry and dissolve them in a little water and add to the mixture. Finally, mix in the diced apple and whipped cream.

■ Cut 1/2 cm slices from the Swiss roll and use them to line 6 small bowls. Fill the bowls with the apple filling and chill overnight.

Before serving, combine all the ingredients for the strawberry sauce and purée.

■ Turn the dishes out on to plates and surround with the sauce.

CLOUDBERRY AND YOGHURT PUDDING

■ Soak the gelatine for 10 minutes, then squeeze dry and dissolve in a little water. Purée the yoghurt with the cloudberries in a liquidiser, foam well and check the purée for sweetness. Add the gelatine liquid, whisk again rapidly and put the mixture in 1–1 1/2 dl bowls.

■ Mix the sugar with the cloudberry purée. When it has dissolved completely, thin the sauce with water to the desired thickness. It is best for it to be fairly thick.

4 SERVINGS	FOR THE CLOUDBERRY SAUCE:
250 G CLOUDBERRIES	150 G PURÉED CLOUDBERRIES
3 DL NATURAL YOGHURT	60 G CASTER SUGAR
4–5 LEAVES GELATINE	A LITTLE WATER, BOILED AND
2–3 TBSP WATER	COOLED
75 G CASTER SUGAR	

125 G CURD CHEESE

A LITTLE BUTTER

3/4 DL AND 1/2 DL SUGAR

1 1/2 TSP CORNFLOUR

2 TBSP VANILLA SUGAR

GRATED RIND OF HALF

A LEMON

1 EGG

1/2 DL MILK

FOR THE CLOUDBERRY SAUCE:

400 G CLOUDBERRIES

150 G SUGAR

4 TBSP CLOUDBERRY LIQUEUR

CURD CHEESE SOUFFLÉ WITH CLOUDBERRY SAUCE

■ Butter 4–5 soufflé dishes carefully. Mix 3/4 dl sugar, the cornflour, vanilla sugar, grated lemon rind, an egg yolk and the milk with the curd cheese.

Whisk the egg white and 1/2 dl sugar until it forms peaks and add the curd cheese mixture, stirring carefully.

Bake at 180°C for about 20 minutes.

■ Purée the cloudberries in a food processor or liquidiser and pass through a sieve.

Mix the sugar and liqueur with the purée. Thin the sauce to the desired thickness with water that you have first boiled and then cooled.

■ Serve the dessert from the soufflé dishes.

SEA BUCKTHORN JELLIED WHITE CHOCOLATE TORTE

■ If buckthorn juice is not available, we suggest a juice obtained by macerating dried apricots in water overnight. Begin the preparation of the buckthorn jelly by soaking the gelatine leaf in water for 10 minutes. Mix the sea buckthorn juice, the water and the sugar. Bring to the boil and remove from the heat. Add the squeezed gelatine. Pour the liquid into a 24 cm dish, place in the refrigerator and leave to set hard.

■ Melt the white chocolate slowly in a bain marie. Put the gelatine leaves to soak in cold water for 10 minutes. Whisk the cream to a soft foam and beat the eggs with an electric beater to a pale foam. Squeeze the gelatine leaves. Place them in the saucepan with the alcohol and heat until they melt. Remove from the heat and set aside. Mix the beaten egg with the chocolate. Add the gelatine-alcohol liquid. Mix until completely smooth. Mix in the whipped cream. Pour into the dish over the buckthorn jelly and level the surface. Cover the dish with film and place in the refrigerator for at least 4 hours.

Dip the base of the dish for a moment in warm water and turn out on a serving dish. Serve as it is or garnished with fruit and berries.

 8–10 SERVINGS

FOR THE BUCKTHORN JELLY:

1 1/2 LEAVES GELATINE
1 DL BUCKTHORN JUICE
1/2 DL WATER
60 G CASTER SUGAR

FOR THE WHITE CHOCOLATE FILLING:

200 G WHITE CHOCOLATE
3 LEAVES GELATINE
5 DL WHIPPING CREAM
2 EGGS
3 TSP RUM
3 TSP TRIPLE SEC LIQUEUR

TASTES

NOT EASILY

FORGOTTEN

Finnish home cooking – or everyday cooking – is simple but good and nourishing. And that is the way we remember it always has been. Mother's vegetable beef soup and grandmother's cabbage rolls remain unforgettable taste experiences all our lives, compared to which, for example, *Soufflé de homard à l'américaine* seems somehow artificial. But in this matter we are undoubtedly all in complete agreement, no matter where in the world we come from and what names our best-loved home dishes carry.

Our Swedish neighbours call their home cooking *husmans-kost*, which originally meant dishes served to servants. Its influences are clearly discernible in many Finnish home dishes, which is of course quite natural if we bear in mind that, until the beginning of the 19th century, Finland was part of the Swedish kingdom. Many recipes from the Russian kitchen have also, through the ages, become part of our own national cuisine.

Indeed, the best feature of our most characteristic national cuisine is its cosmopolitan quality and its admirable capacity to absorb influences from outside. Without these, our everyday dinner tables would be much the poorer. And it is to a great extent thanks to them that the most 'Finnish' gastronomic cuisine survives, full of vitality, from one decade to another. As proof, the example of the above-mentioned cabbage rolls will suffice. For they originally came to us from Turkey – although with the gentle assistance of our western neighbour.

■ Place the burbot liver in a generous quantity of cold water for an hour. Then simmer for 10–15 minutes in water seasoned with sea salt until cooked through, and leave to stand in the cooking liquid.

Remove the head and all the fins from the burbot. Place them in cold water with the coarse salt. Bring to the boil and remove the froth that forms on the surface. Add half the onion, finely sliced, and the peppercorns and bay leaf to the liquid. Simmer gently for 15 minutes.

BURBOT SOUP

4—6 SERVINGS		
	1—2 ONIONS	
	8 ALLSPICE PEPPERCORNS	
1 KG BURBOT, SKINNED AND CLEANED,	1 BAY LEAF	
WITH LIVER	400 G POTATOES, PEELED	
1 L WATER	60 G BUTTER	
SEA SALT	(DILL)	

Cut the burbot crosswise into 5 cm pieces and add them to the liquid. Add water as necessary. Cook at boiling point for 10 minutes or until the burbot is cooked through. Remove the saucepan from the heat and cool for about ten minutes – do not stir. Remove the burbot pieces with a slotted spoon and sieve the liquid.

Remove the burbot flesh from the bone and cut into spoon-sized pieces. Check the saltiness of the cooking liquid.

Place the potatoes, cut into 1 1/2 cm dices, in the liquid and simmer until tender. Finally, add the burbot pieces, bring to the boil and add the butter.

■ Slice the liver and place in soup plates, pour the soup over and sprinkle raw onion (and, if you wish, finely chopped dill) over.

WHITEFISH SOUP FROM SATAKUNTA

4 SERVINGS	
	6 DL WATER
	25 G SEA SALT
A WHITEFISH WEIGHING ABOUT 1.2 KG	8 ALLSPICE PEPPERCORNS
600 G POTATOES	2 BAY LEAVES
1 ONION	50 G BUTTER
	1 TBSP DILL

■ Place the sliced potatoes and chopped onion in a saucepan. Add the water and salt.

Cut the cleaned and scaled whitefish crossways into slices about 2 cm thick. Pile the slices on top of the potatoes.

Simmer gently, carefully removing the froth that forms on the surface. Add the seasonings and simmer for about 1 hour. Finally, add the butter and finely chopped dill.

■ Serve the soup straight from the saucepan. Sour-dough rye bread is the usual accompaniment.

PEA SOUP & SHROVE TUESDAY BUNS

4 SERVINGS	**4** SERVINGS
3 DL DRIED PEAS	4 ROUND BUNS
1 1/2 DL WATER	ALMOND PASTE
500 G BREAST OF PORK	3 DL WHIPPED CREAM
1—2 TSP SALT	8 DL MILK

■ Rinse the peas carefully in cold water. Place the peas in a saucepan, add the water and soak them overnight.

Bring the peas to the boil in their soaking water and add the meat, cut into 3 cm cubes. Add the salt and simmer on a medium heat for at least 3 hours. Add water if necessary.

■ Cut a 'cap' from the tops of each bun. Scoop out the inside of the buns and moisten with a drop of milk. Fill the buns with the almond paste and the whipped cream. Replace the cap.

■ Serve with hot milk. Instead of the almond paste, you can fill the buns with strawberry jam and whipped cream. Buns with this filling are usually served plain, for example with coffee.

VENDACE CASSEROLE

4 SERVINGS		25 G BUTTER
		1 TSP SALT
1 KG VENDACE		5 DL WATER
1 LEEK		10 WHOLE WHITE PEPPERCORNS
85 G BACON SLICES		2 BAY LEAVES

■ Clean the vendace but do not remove their heads.

Cut the leeks into rounds and the bacon into strips. Fry the bacon strips for a moment in a frying pan.

Butter an ovenproof dish and pile in the vendace and leek-bacon mixture, in layers. Sprinkle a little salt on each layer. Finally, pour the water over and add the peppercorns and the bay leaves. Bake at 175°C for 1 hour.

■ Serve with puréed potatoes.

BOILED PIKE WITH EGG SAUCE

4 SERVINGS	FOR THE EGG SAUCE:
	40 G BUTTER
1.3–1.5 KG PIKE	40 G FLOUR
WATER AND COARSE SALT	1/2 L MILK
1 ONION, FINELY SLICED	1 DL COOKING LIQUID FROM THE PIKE
1 CARROT, FINELY SLICED	SALT AND FRESHLY GROUND WHITE PEPPER
PIECE OF THE GREEN PART OF A LEEK	100 G EGG, BOILED AND FINELY CHOPPED
1 BAY LEAF	4 TBSP DILL, FINELY CHOPPED
5 ALLSPICE PEPPERCORNS AND	
5 WHITE PEPPERCORNS	

■ Remove the scales from the pike, clean it and wash it well, and remove the head and tail. Cut the fish into four equal-sized pieces.

Place the pieces, the head (wash it first and remove the gills) and the tail in a saucepan. Cover with water. Add salt.

Bring to the boil and remove the froth that appears on the surface. Add the vegetables, the bay leaves and the peppercorns. Simmer for about 15–20 minutes until tender.

■ Melt the butter and stew the butter in it for a couple of minutes. Allow the mixture to brown.

Add the heated milk in a couple of stages and whisk the mixture until it is smooth.

Finally, add the sieved pike stock and simmer the sauce for 10 minutes. Season with salt and pepper.

Mix the egg and dill into the sauce and heat. If necessary, use the remaining pike stock to thin the sauce. Take the pike pieces from the stock and drain well before serving.

■ Serve with boiled potatoes.

BAKED BREAM

4 SERVINGS

ONE BREAM WEIGHING 1 1/2 KG

SALT AND WHITE PEPPER

3 SPRIGS OF DILL

1 DL WHITE BREADCRUMBS,

FRESH OR DRIED

2 DL CREAM

60 G BUTTER

■ Scale and clean the bream. Rinse and dry it well on kitchen paper.

Rub salt and pepper on the inner and outer surfaces of the fish. Place the sprigs of dill inside the fish.

■ Grate some fresh, crustless bread. Place the bream in a buttered oven dish.

Make decorative cuts on the outer surface of the fish in parallel or in a chequered pattern. Pour the cream over the fish and sprinkle the breadcrumbs over. Place pats of butter over the breadcrumbs to give the fish a good colour in the oven.

Bake the fish at 170°C, basting it with butter during cooking. The fish is ready when its surface is a good brown colour and the cream has thickened into a sauce.

■ Serve immediately, hot from the oven dish.

BALTIC HERRING WITH POTATOES

PER PERSON:

200 G SALTED BALTIC HERRINGS, UNGUTTED

WATER

2 LARGE POTATOES, UNPEELED

1/4 ONION, FINELY SLICED

3 ALLSPICE PEPPERCORNS

■ Place the herrings in a generous quantity of cold water to soak for 24 hours. Cut the potatoes in half, place in a saucepan and add enough water just to cover the potatoes.

Place the sliced onion, peppercorns and Baltic herrings over the potatoes so that the potatoes are completely covered. Cover and simmer until the potatoes are tender.

■ Pour the water away and serve in the cooking dish with butter, white sauce or white onion sauce.

BLOOD PANCAKES

4 SERVINGS		1 SMALL ANCHOVY FILLET
		A LITTLE MARJORAM
2 1/2 DL BLOOD		GROUND WHITE AND BLACK PEPPER
1 SMALL ONION, FINELY CHOPPED		SALT
BUTTER		CLEAR MELTED BUTTER FOR FRYING
100 G PORK FAT, CUT INTO TINY CUBES		
2 1/2 DL RYE FLOUR		**FOR THE LINGONBERRY PURÉE:**
1 1/1 DL WHEAT FLOUR		200 G LINGONBERRIES
2 EGGS		50–60 G CASTER SUGAR
2 1/2 DL PILSNER BEER		

■ Crush the lingonberries and sugar carefully together with a wooden spoon or potato masher.

■ Fry the onion in a little butter until done and set aside.

Fry the cubes of pork fat in a dry pan so that the fat runs, but do not brown.

Set aside and cool to room temperature.

Sieve the blood. Whisk in both types of flour and the eggs and, separately, the Pilsner, the finely chopped anchovy fillet, the seasonings, the onion and the pork with its fat. Finally, add the salt and allow the batter to rest for an hour before cooking.

Before you begin to make the pancakes, mix the batter once more. Make crisp pancakes in a pancake pan using the clear melted butter.

■ Serve with melted butter and the sweetened lingonberry purée.

LIVER CASSEROLE

6 SERVINGS		1 ONION
		50 G BUTTER
1/2 L WATER		SALT AND GROUND WHITE PEPPER
SALT		MARJORAM
2 DL PUDDING RICE		A LITTLE GROUND ALLSPICE
1/2 DL MILK		ABOUT 8 DL MILK
		1 EGG
400 G MINCED BEEF OR		3 TBSP SYRUP
PORK LIVER		2 DL RAISINS

■ Bring the water and salt to the boil, add the rice and simmer.

When the mixture begins to thicken, add all the milk, little by little, until the rice is almost done. Simmer for 20–25 minutes, take the saucepan off the heat and set aside.

Fry the finely chopped onion in a little butter until it is done and mix it with the rice pudding. Mix in all the seasonings, the cold milk, the whisked egg, the minced liver, the syrup and the raisins. Check the seasoning.

Butter a suitable oven dish, pour the mixture in and bake at 180°C for about 1 1/2 hours.

■ Serve melted butter and sweetened lingonberry purée (see above) with the liver casserole.

CABBAGE ROLLS

6 SERVINGS	
	1 DL PUDDING RICE, BOILED
	2 EGGS
1 SMALL OR MEDIUM SPRING CABBAGE	GROUND WHITE AND
WATER, SALT	BLACK PEPPER
400 G PORK-BEEF MINCE	A LITTLE MARJORAM
1 SMALL ONION, FINELY CHOPPED	ABOUT 1 1/2 DL CREAM
1 DL INNER LEAVES OF	SYRUP AND
THE CABBAGE, FINELY CHOPPED	MELTED BUTTER
BUTTER FOR FRYING	A LITTLE MEAT STOCK

■ Scoop the base of the cabbage away and remove the outer leaves if necessary. Simmer in salted water. Take the leaves out of the saucepan as they become tender. Do not overcook them. Drain the leaves and smooth down their veins.

■ Mix with the mince the finely chopped, fried onion, the finely chopped cabbage, rice, eggs and seasonings, and enough cream to make a loosish mixture.

Spread the cabbage leaves out on a table and place about 50 g of the stuffing on each. Wrap the leaves around the filling to make a pillow-like parcel and pack them tightly into a buttered oven dish. Sprinkle the parcels with syrup and melted butter.

Begin baking them at 250°C. When the parcels have clearly browned, turn them over. Sprinkle lightly with syrup and melted butter and allow the other side to brown.

Turn once more, add a little meat stock to the dish and cover tightly with aluminium foil. Braise for at least 1 hour at 130°C, until the parcels are completely tender and succulent.

■ Serve with boiled potatoes, the cooking juices or melted butter and sweetened lingonberry purée (see page 88).

MOOSE MEAT-BALLS

4 SERVINGS	
	BUTTER
	1 LARGE ONION, FINELY CHOPPED
400 G MINCED MOOSE-MEAT	SALT AND WHITE PEPPER
200 G FATTY PORK MINCE	SPRIG OF FRESH THYME
1 EGG	
1 DL WHIPPING CREAM	**FOR THE SAUCE:**
1/2 DL WATER	2 DL GOOD GAME STOCK
50 G WHITE BREAD,	2 DL WHIPPING CREAM
CRUSTS REMOVED	1 TBSP BUTTER-FLOUR THICKENING

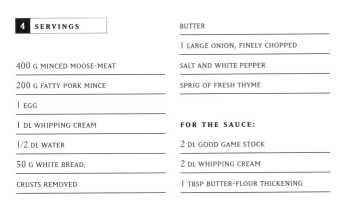

■ Mix the two types of mince and add the bread, which has been allowed to absorb the water and cream, and the onion, which you have glazed in butter. Season the mixture and add liquid as necessary. Add the thyme leaves (not the stems). Check the seasoning and fry a small experimental meat-ball.

Form the mince mixture into balls and fry in butter until brown.

■ Simmer the game stock and whipping cream together. Add the butter-flour thickening and continue to simmer until the mixture has thickened.

■ Serve with puréed potatoes and sweetened lingonberry purée (see page 88).

PORK IN GRAVY

5–6 SERVINGS

1 KG BONED PORK (SIDE)

3 ONIONS, ABOUT 400 G

1 TBSP BUTTER

1 DL FLOUR

1 L WATER

6 ALLSPICE PEPPERCORNS, CRUSHED

SALT

■ Cut the pork into strips about 1/2 cm wide and 10 cm long.

Brown the strips in a hot pan. Pour the browned meat into a sieve and reserve the fat in a saucepan. Finally, brown the finely sliced onion.

Add the butter and flour to the fat in the saucepan. Cook over a medium heat until the flour is dark brown in colour. Add the browned onions, meat, water and seasonings.

■ Simmer on medium heat for 2 hours. Serve with puréed potatoes and sliced pickled cucumber.

BILBERRY SOUP

4 SERVINGS

1 L FRESH BILBERRIES

1 L WATER

1 1/2 DL SUGAR

2 TBSP POTATO FLOUR

■ Simmer the bilberries in water until all the flavour has come out of the berries. Sieve the mixture.

Add sugar to the liquid and thicken with the potato flour, dissolved in a little water.

■ Bring the soup to the boil once more. Serve hot or cold.

BARLEY PORAGE AND RAISIN SOUP

4 SERVINGS

FOR THE BARLEY PORAGE:	FOR THE RAISIN SOUP:
2 DL PEARL BARLEY	1 PACKET RAISINS (250 G)
2 L MILK	1 DL SUGAR
1 TSP SALT	1 L WATER
50 G BUTTER	2 TBSP POTATO FLOUR

■ Soak the pearl barley in a saucepan in a little water overnight.

Set the saucepan on the heat and add, at first, 1 l of the milk. Simmer, mixing from time to time.

Add milk when necessary and continue to simmer. The flavour of the porage improves the longer you cook it. A successful result demands at least 3 hours' cooking.

You can also bake the porage in the oven, at a medium heat. When it is almost done, add the salt and butter.

■ Pour 1 l water into a saucepan and soak the raisins for at least 3 hours. Set the saucepan on the heat, bring to the boil, and add the sugar.

Dissolve the potato flour in a little water and thicken the soup, mixing carefully.

■ Serve warm by itself, or cold with hot barley porage.

BAKED CHEESE MADE WITH BEESTINGS

4 SERVINGS

1 TSP BUTTER
1/2 TSP SALT
1 L BEESTINGS
GROUND CINNAMON AND SUGAR

■ Butter an oven dish of about 1 1/2 l capacity. Mix the salt with the beestings. Pour the mixture into the dish and bake at 200 °C for 35–40 minutes.

■ Serve with ground cinnamon and sugar.

WINTER

IN THE HOME
OF THE
REINDEER,
WINTER COMES
EARLY

The first snow often falls on the hills of northern Finland as early as October. As the snow arrives, the willow grouse exchanges its colourful brown summer plumage for a brilliant white winter costume. For the willow grouse, this camouflage colouring is a question of life or death, for it is perhaps the most sought-after and delicious of Finnish game birds.

Willow grouse is not daily fare even in its home territory. The willow grouse stocks of the north have declined continuously, and trapping them in metre-deep snow and 30 degrees of frost is slow and difficult work. Winter willow grouse usually arrives in the shops frozen. It is unusual game in this respect, too, for in practice it freezes itself. A willow grouse trapped in a harsh frost freezes instantly when dead. In its coat of feathers and down, it keeps excellently in the freezer for quite a few months. The bird is plucked and cleaned only when it is ready for cooking.

Reindeer are nowadays slaughtered when less than a year old, when their meat is at its most tender and fine in colour. Cold-smoked reindeer meat, the pride of the reindeer-breeders of Lapland, is already widely known outside Finland. Its fame is probably exceeded only by that of reindeer stew with potato butter, or Lapp potato stew, and crushed lingonberries (page 88). The best place to be served reindeer stew is in an open tent in Lapland proper — preferably by a Sámi cook.

If you number any keen huntsmen among your circle of friends, you may yet one day have the pleasure of tasting proper, homemade hare stew made from hare macerated in buttermilk though other marinades are also popular.

The hare was once a very common game animal throughout Finland. With the decrease in hunting as part of a normal way of life, the hare has almost completely disappeared from the Finnish dining table. Fortunately, the best restaurants succeed from time to time in procuring it for their menus, and the markets of major cities often have frozen hares in stock.

Soups containing generous quantities of root vegetables and meat or sausage — generally accompanied by dark bread — are common winter lunch dishes, as are fish soups, which are often made on a milk base.

Pea soup (page 85) has its own, quite distinct place in Finnish culture. It has fed armies from one generation to another. And it is difficult to imagine any winter sporting event or public festival without a steaming 'soup kitchen' in the midst of the thronging masses.

Pea soup is generally followed by the same traditional desserts. The speciality for Shrove Tuesday is a bun filled with almond paste and whipped cream, which is eaten with warm milk. Pancakes, fried or baked in the oven, round off a weekday lunch of pea soup which, according to the old custom, is always served on Thursdays.

The meat of the willow grouse is fine-textured and has a strong taste of pure game that should not be masked by strong flavours. Willow grouse is quick-cooking and its flavour is at its finest when the meat remains a handsome pink in colour.

If there were a competition for the best domesticated animal, reindeer would be among the winners. Despite the fact that, in reality, it is a rather unusual hybrid of domesticated and game animal.

It differs from other domesticated animals in the fact that it grazes all year round and seeks out its food for itself. It is mainly for this reason that reindeer meat develops its characteristically fine gamey flavour.

UNDER THE ICE HIDES AN UGLY, CURIOUS FISH

Finns will recognise the fish as the burbot. In days gone by, the supposed curiosity of the fish was exploited cunningly in catching it. At the time of the clear ice of mid-winter, the mud-lurking burbot was tempted to the surface by hitting the ice with a wooden club. When the fish was visible under the ice, it was 'clobbered' unconscious by hitting the ice immediately above it hard with the club. The fish was then lifted out of the water through a hole made in the ice.

The burbot is a typical seasonal fish of Finland's inland waterways. The best catches are made in mid-winter, in January and February. The burbot, which generally weighs less than two kilograms, is certainly no beauty. Naturally greenish or yellowish brown, and slimy, the fish is generally available from fishmongers ready skinned, which has understandably increased the popularity of this otherwise excellent fish.

The burbot is at its best in simple traditional foods, soups and stews.

On the west coast, burbot soup is generally thickened with cream or milk, while along the eastern border rye flour mixed with water is added to the clear soup and, finally, chopped raw onion.

Burbot liver and roe are acknowledged as great delicacies. The liver is generally eaten as an accompaniment to a roe stew, but another common way of presenting it is to serve chopped liver together with roe and blinis.

W inter catches are very variable. Most commonly available are pike-perch, perch and whitefish and, of course, rainbow trout and salmon. Baltic herring and vendace also make regular appearances on the winter table.

Professional winter fishing is hard work, but for tens of thousands of Sunday anglers it is nothing short of a passion, and the best way to relax and enjoy the peace of the countryside. Even poor catches cannot prevent the dedicated ice angler from making his way, weekend after weekend, to his favourite hole in the ice, as long as the ice will carry his weight.

BUT THIS IS *really* DELICIOUS!

Roe is the Finns' caviar. Cheaper, it's true, but at is best, many people think, tastier than the best Russian caviar. Roe is a typically

seasonal dish. Burbot roe makes a handsome beginning to the season. Indeed, in January and February, burbot roe with its accompaniments is to be found on the menu of almost every self-respecting restaurant.

It is relatively difficult to remove the membranes and veins that surround the close-grained burbot roe. Thus it is also the most expensive of the roes. If, on the other hand, one is pre-

The season of the less well-known ruffe and Baltic herring roes is later in the spring.

Ruffe roe has always been a highly prized delicacy – it is said that, during tsarist times, it was continually sent to the royal buffet tables of St Petersburg.

Rainbow trout roe is on offer all year round. Because of its reasonable price, it is commonly found on more ordinary tables, served either on its own or as a flavouring for sauces. Rainbow trout roe is equally at home in a spring asparagus sauce and in the dishes of the Christmas table.

The season for vendace and whitefish roe takes place in autumn. Vendace roe, often called Finnish caviar, is, many people believe, the absolute king of roes. And it has also become highly valued outside Finnish national waters, too. The roe of the lake vendace is a fine orange-red, while the roe of the sea vendace is paler and reminiscent of whitefish roe. Generally both are served lightly salted, like burbot roe.

An orthodox roe dish requires, in addition to burbot, vendace, whitefish or rainbow trout roe, generous quantities of white and red onion, and soured cream that has been mixed until it is runny. Boiled and chopped burbot liver and chopped dill are excellent accompaniments to burbot roe. Many people recommend whipped cream instead of soured cream to go with the mild-flavoured burbot roe. The roes are eaten with blinis made from buckwheat or wheat flour or toast.

'Properly fried blinis are light, fluffy and a beautiful brown in colour. They absorb melted butter and soured cream like sponges and become juicy and glossy.'

Such is the lyricism with which a true expert in real Russian blinis describes these excellent pancakes. After which a chilled measure of vodka may be just the thing! Recipes for flavoured vodkas are on pages 31–33.

pared to take the trouble to clean the roe oneself, one can buy a plump burbot roe at the same time as a generous burbot starter for almost the price of just the fish. Before enjoying burbot roe, it is recommended to freeze it to kill any possible tapeworm. Many a real gourmand cannot countenance this, but is prepared to take a small risk and to enjoy his roe fresh, and lightly salted.

6 SERVINGS

200 G COLD-SMOKED REINDEER MEAT

3 LEAVES GELATINE

WATER

APPROX. 100 G SOUR-DOUGH CRISPBREAD

3 DL MEAT STOCK

3 DL WHIPPING CREAM

2 DL SOURED CREAM

3 TBSP PARSLEY, CHOPPED

1 TSP MUSTARD

1/2 TSP GROUND WHITE PEPPER

SMOKED REINDEER CAKE

■ Begin by soaking the gelatine leaves in cold water for about half an hour. Moisten the crispbread in 2 dl of the meat stock. Whisk the whipping cream and soured cream to a foam. Cut the reindeer meat into small cubes or pass them through a mincer.

Press all the water out of the gelatine leaves and dissolve them in 1 dl of hot meat stock. Let the mixture cool.

Add the parsley, mustard, white pepper, cubed reindeer meat and meat stock to the whipped cream.

Line a loose-based dish (20 cm in diameter) with the crispbread. Fill the dish with the smoked reindeer mixture and place it in a refrigerator to set for about 12 hours.

■ Serve with a green salad.

PICKLED CUCUMBER
WITH HONEY BUTTER AND SOURED CREAM

■ Whip the soured cream until it forms a foam and divide among the plates.

Cut the cucumbers lengthways into four.

Melt the butter in a pan, add the cucumber pieces and warm on a gentle heat.

Place the cucumbers on the plates and add the honey to the pan. Heat until the honey has completely melted.

■ Pour the honey butter over the cucumbers and serve immediately.

A measure of chilled vodka is the natural accompaniment to this Russian-type starter.

4 SERVINGS

4 PICKLED CUCUMBERS

3 TBSP SOURED CREAM

3 TBSP BUTTER

3 TBSP HONEY

10 SERVINGS

FOR THE PASTRY:

2 1/2–3 DL WATER

10 G YEAST

SALT

300 G FLOUR

300 G WHOLEMEAL FLOUR

100 G POTATO PURÉE

FOR THE FILLING:

60 G PUDDING RICE

1/2 L MILK

SALT

1 TSP BUTTER

FOR THE BASIL BUTTER:

80 G BUTTER AT ROOM

TEMPERATURE

16 BASIL LEAVES, FINELY

CHOPPED

A FEW DROPS OF

LEMON JUICE

A LITTLE FRESHLY GROUND

BLACK PEPPER

SALT (IF YOU ARE USING

UNSALTED BUTTER)

GOAT´S CHEESE

USE A ROUND FRENCH

GOAT´S CHEESE

GRATINATED ROUNDELS WITH GOAT'S CHEESE AND BASIL BUTTER

■ Warm the water to blood temperature, dissolve the yeast in it, add the salt and mix in both types of flour and the potato purée. Cover with a cloth and allow to rest at room temperature for about 1 hour. Rinse the rice in a sieve under running water, shake. Bring 2 dl milk to the boil, add the rice and boil until thick, stirring occasionally. Add 2 dl milk and boil until thick once more, mixing at the same time. Add the rest of the milk and the salt and butter and boil to a loose porage. Take the saucepan off the heat and cool. The total cooking time is about 25 minutes.

■ Knead the pastry and roll it out thin. Then let the rolled-out pastry rest on the working surface for 5–10 minutes; cut 10 cm discs. Place the discs on a baking tray covered with baking paper. Mix the porage well and spread it on top of the discs in an even 2 mm layer. Bake in a 250°C oven for about 15 minutes or until the rounds are a light golden-brown at the edges.

■ Cream the butter until it turns pale; add the chopped basil, the lemon juice and the black pepper (and salt, if necessary). Brush the rounds well with the basil butter, place a slice of goat's cheese on top and place under the grill until the surface of the cheese is lightly browned.

■ Serve immediately with, for example, cold-smoked salmon or a small salad. To drink: with salmon a Gewürztraminer, otherwise mineral water or a Saumur.

BURBOT PIECES AND VEGETABLES WITH SEA BUCKTHORN SAUCE

■ Clean the burbot fillet, remove all the bones and cut it into strips the width of your little finger. Season the strips with salt and pepper and place them in a buttered dish with the coriander stalks. Add 3 tbsp water. Cover the dish tightly with aluminium foil and bake in a 220°C oven (5 minutes if the dish is a metal one, 8 minutes if it is earthenware). Remove the dish from the oven and leave the fish strips to rest under the foil for about four minutes; then cool them.

Cut the carrots and broccoli florets diagonally into thin discs. Wash the split leek thoroughly and cut it, too, diagonally into strips about 1 cm wide. Blanch all of the vegetables separately until tender in water seasoned with sea salt, cool in cold water and drain well.

■ Mix the sugar, a little salt and pepper with the sea buckthorn juice. Vigorously whisk in the rape-seed oil, then the clabbered cream, mixing just enough to make it combine with the sauce (whisking too strongly would thicken the sauce).

■ Make a bed of salad leaves on each plate. Place the pieces of burbot, the vegetable strips and the coriander leaves into a large mixing bowl. Pour the sauce over and mix the ingredients carefully together. Place on top of the salad leaves.

A medium-dry, acidic Gewürztraminer makes a good complement to the combination of flavours of the burbot and the sea buckthorn sauce.

4–6 SERVINGS

500 G BURBOT FILLET

SALT AND PEPPER FROM THE MILL

3–4 SPRIGS OF FRESH CORIANDER, LEAVES STRIPPED

3 TBSP WATER

100 G SMALL CARROTS, PEELED

100 G BROCCOLI FLORETS

70 G LEEKS

SEA SALT

ASSORTED SALAD LEAVES

FOR THE SEA BUCKTHORN SAUCE:

2 1/2 DL UNSWEETENED SEA BUCKTHORN JUICE OR JUICE OBTAINED BY SOAKING DRIED APRICOTS IN WATER OVERNIGHT

1 TSP CASTER SUGAR

SALT AND PEPPER

3 TBSP RAPE-SEED OIL

6 TBSP CLABBERED CREAM

6 SERVINGS

600 g CELERY	
1 L WATER	
1 TSP SALT	
2 DL CREAM	
NUTMEG	
3 DL DRY CHAMPAGNE	
A PINCH OF WHITE PEPPER	
2 DL WHIPPING CREAM	

CELERY-CHAMPAGNE SOUP

■ Peel and cube the celery. Boil in salted water until tender.

Place the celery in a liquidiser and purée. Pour back into the saucepan and add the cream. Grate a little nutmeg over.

Boil for a moment and then add the champagne, whisking constantly. Add the pepper and check the salt.

■ Pour into individual oven-proof dishes. Place the whipped cream on top. Grill in the oven until the surface takes on a fine brown colour.

FENNEL AND POTATO SOUP WITH GARLIC SOURED CREAM

■ Cut the onion and fennel into very thin slices and stew them, without browning, in 2 tbsp olive oil on a medium heat for 5 minutes.

Add the fish stock and the cubed potatoes, the bay leaf, the star anise and a little sea salt. Simmer gently, almost covered, for 20–30 minutes.

Remove the bay leaf and the star anise. Pour the soup into a liquidiser and purée well. Pour back into the saucepan, heat and season with the cayenne pepper until 'hot'.

Mix 2 tbsp olive oil with the soured cream and the crushed garlic cloves.

■ Place the soured cream mixture in warmed soup plates and pour the soup over. Mix with a fork so that the soup becomes slightly stripy. Garnish with chopped fennel leaves.

A good accompaniment to this soup would be a dry Spanish or Provençal rosé wine.

4 SERVINGS

200 G FRESH FENNEL, CLEANED

1 SMALL ONION

4 TBSP GREEN OLIVE OIL

1 L FISH STOCK

4 MEDIUM-SIZED POTATOES, PEELED

HALF A BAY LEAF

1 STAR ANISE

SEA SALT

A LITTLE CAYENNE PEPPER

4 CLOVES GARLIC

500 G REINDEER BONES

500 G BONELESS SHOULDER OF REINDEER

1 TSP COARSE SALT

3 L WATER

1 TSP WHOLE ALLSPICE PEPPERCORNS

2 BAY LEAVES

2 CARROTS

100 G CELERY, PEELED

2 ONIONS

400 G POTATOES

2 TBSP BUTTER

1 DL PEARL BARLEY

3 TBSP PARSLEY, CHOPPED

REINDEER SOUP

■ Place the reindeer bones, shoulder and salt in a saucepan. Add the water. Heat the saucepan, and carefully remove the foam that appears on the surface. Boil for about two hours, until the meat is tender.

Remove the meat from the saucepan and pass the stock through a sieve.

Cut the peeled vegetables into cubes and the onions into segments. Melt the butter in the saucepan and stew the pearl barley in it for about 10 minutes. Add the vegetables and onion and continue to stew for a moment. Pour the stock into the saucepan and cook until tender.

Finally, add the cubed shoulder of reindeer and the chopped parsley.

■ Serve immediately with warm bread.

PARSLEY SOUP
WITH PORK SAUSAGES

■ Place all the stock ingredients in a suitable saucepan and simmer gently for 45 minutes. Pass the stock through a fine sieve. You need 1 litre of the stock.

■ Heat the stock, add the bay leaf and simmer the courgettes in the stock for one minute. Then remove the courgettes, add the kohlrabi or swede and simmer for a couple of minutes. Finally, cook the carrots in the same way.

Make the pork sausages into small, fingertip-sized balls between your fore-finger and middle finger and simmer them in the stock until they are cooked. Set them aside and cover with kitchen film.

Cut the potatoes into large cubes and boil them in the stock until tender. Remove the bay leaf and pour the stock into a liquidiser; purée until very fine. Sieve the soup back into the saucepan and bring to the boil. Mix the starch in a little water and add it to the boiling soup. Simmer for another minute or two and season with salt and pepper. Thin, if necessary, with water.

■ Place the cubes of cheese, vegetables and sausage balls in the soup plates. Pour the stock over and, finally, sprinkle with the chopped parsley.

6 SERVINGS

FOR THE STOCK:
50 G ONION, CHOPPED
50 G LEEKS, CUT INTO THIN STRIPS
30 G CELERY, FINELY DICED
30 G CARROTS, FINELY DICED
1 DL PARSLEY, CHOPPED
1/2 L WATER

200–250 G PORK SAUSAGES
1 L VEGETABLE STOCK
1 BAY LEAF

30 G COURGETTES, CUT INTO SMALL CUBES
40 G KOHLRABI OR SWEDE, CUT INTO SMALL CUBES
40 G CARROTS, CUT INTO SMALL CUBES
2 MEDIUM-SIZED POTATOES
2 TSP BARLEY- OR CORNFLOUR
WATER
SALT AND PEPPER
40 G STRONG EMMENTHAL CHEESE, CUT INTO SMALL CUBES
1 DL PARSLEY, CHOPPED

4 SERVINGS

4 PIKE-PERCH FILLETS

OF 150–170 G, SKINNED

3 TBSP GROUND MUSHROOMS

4 TBSP GROUND ALMONDS

SALT

1 EGG YOLK

BUTTER FOR FRYING

FOR THE WINE VINEGAR SAUCE:

120 G BUTTER

2 TBSP SHERRY VINEGAR

FILLET OF PIKE-PERCH FINISHED WITH GROUND MUSHROOM AND ALMOND IN A WARM WINE VINEGAR SAUCE

■ Clean the pike-perch fillets. Mix the ground mushrooms and almonds together thoroughly. Season the fillets with salt. Brush one side lightly with the egg yolk and sprinkle with the mushroom-almond powder so that the fillet is evenly covered.

■ Heat the butter you have reserved for frying until it is nut-brown and pass it through a very fine sieve or muslin into a small saucepan and add the sherry vinegar.

■ Heat the butter in a non-stick frying pan until it is a pale nut-colour. Fry the pike-perch fillets until done, the mushroom-almond side first.

Heat the sauce to about 60°C, whisking constantly.

■ Place the pikeperch fillets on plates, and pour a little sauce beside each. Serve with, for example, steamed green vegetables.

A good accompaniment would be a medium full-bodied white from Burgundy, for example a Mâcon, or a Petit Chablis.

BALTIC HERRING FILLETS
WITH A MILD GREEN PEPPER BUTTER

■ Clean the Baltic herrings and fillet them; cut off the dorsal fins. Toast the green peppercorns in a dry non-stick pan until they are dry. Then pour the vodka over and flambé. Allow to cool. Cream the butter until pale, mix in the green peppercorns and the dill. Butter a low roasting tin (about 22–24 cm in diameter) thoroughly and sprinkle 1 tbsp breadcrumbs on the base. Heat the oven to 220°C.

Season the Baltic herring fillets with salt. Fold them in half, skin side up; press lightly. Layer the fillets in the tin, interleaving them in the form of a flower. Sprinkle the green peppercorns over as evenly as possible and, finally, sprinkle over all the remaining breadcrumbs.

Bake in the oven for 20–25 minutes, until the surface is crispy and well gratinated.

■ Serve at once while still hot with puréed potatoes.

To drink, you could serve water or beer accompanied by a measure of cold vodka, as the Finns do. A suitable wine alternative would be an Italian white from Soave.

4 — 6 SERVINGS

1.2 KG BALTIC HERRINGS OR 600 G BALTIC HERRING FILLETS

2 TSP PRESERVED GREEN PEPPERCORNS

1 TBSP FINLANDIA VODKA

100 G SOFT BUTTER

2 TBSP CHOPPED DILL

1 TBSP BUTTER TO GREASE ROASTING TRAY

4 TBSP BREADCRUMBS

SALT

4 SERVINGS

800 G VENDACE

SALT AND WHITE PEPPER

3 TBSP BREADCRUMBS

5 TBSP FLOUR

BUTTER FOR FRYING

SPRIGS OF DILL

FOR THE STEWED LEEKS:

150 G LEEKS

2 TSP BUTTER

1 TBSP FLOUR

1 DL CREAM

1 1/2 DL SOURED CREAM

SALT AND WHITE PEPPER

FOR THE WAFER:

200 G PUFF PASTRY

1 EGG YOLK FOR GLAZING

200 G VENDACE ROE

VENDACE AND VENDACE ROE WITH A LEEK WAFER

■ This dish can also be made with gudgeons or fresh sardines.

■ Open and clean the vendace and rinse them in cold water. Dry them on kitchen paper and season with salt and finely ground white pepper. Mix the breadcrumbs with the flour and roll the vendace in the mixture, one by one.

■ Split the leek lengthways and wash it well in cold water. Cut into thin strips. Melt the butter in a frying pan and add the leek strips. Cook for a moment and add the flour, mix until smooth. Add the cream and soured cream, season with salt and pepper. Cook on a medium heat for 10 minutes.

■ Roll the puff pastry out to a thickness of 1/2 cm and cut into four squares. Brush the squares with egg yolk and bake at 175°C until they are a handsome brown colour.

Fry the vendace on a low heat on both sides until crisp. Split the wafers and fill them with the stewed leek and vendace roe.

■ Put the vendace on plates and, next to them, the filled wafer. Garnish with sprigs of dill.

To drink, light beer or mineral water is the best choice.

SMOKED BURBOT LIVERS AND WILD MUSHROOM ROULADE WITH MILK SAUCE

■ Melt the butter in a saucepan and add the flour. Add the hot full cream milk and simmer on a medium heat for 10 minutes. Season with salt and whisk in the egg yolks. Cool until cold. Add the stiffly whipped whites and pour the mixture on to a baking tray lined with baking paper. Cook in a 175°C oven for 15–20 minutes.

■ Soften the leek in butter. Add the wild mushrooms, cut into small dice, and the soured cream. Season with the white pepper and, if necessary, the salt. Spread the warm mushroom filling on the omelette and roll it into a tight roulade. Cut the roulade into slices just before serving.

■ Remove the veins from the surface of the burbot livers and rinse them in cold water. Heat 1 l water in a saucepan and add the chopped onion and seasonings. Boil for 10 minutes and add the livers. Simmer for another 5 minutes and then remove the livers from the liquid. Season the livers with salt and smoke them until done in a smoking box.

■ Melt the butter in a saucepan. Add the flour and mix until smooth. Pour in the hot milk and simmer the sauce for 10 minutes on a medium heat, stirring from time to time.

Beer is a good choice, as are a Pinot Gris from Alsace or a dry sherry.

---

4 SERVINGS

FOR THE WILD MUSHROOM ROULADE:

50 G BUTTER

1/2 DL FLOUR

4 DL FULL CREAM MILK

1 TSP SALT

4 EGG YOLKS

4 EGG WHITES

FOR THE FILLING:

1 LEEK, FINELY SLICED

1 TBSP BUTTER

300 G WILD MUSHROOMS, BLANCHED

3 TBSP SOURED CREAM OR CRÈME FRAÎCHE

GROUND WHITE PEPPER, SALT

FOR THE SMOKED BURBOT LIVERS:

400 G BURBOT LIVERS

1 L WATER

1 ONION

SALT AND BLACK PEPPER

2 BAY LEAVES

FOR THE MILK SAUCE:

2 TBSP BUTTER

3 TBSP FLOUR

1/2 L MILK

SALT AND WHITE PEPPER

4 SERVINGS	FOR THE HORSE-RADISH SAUCE:
1 KG BONELESS BRISKET OF BEEF	50 G BUTTER
1 TSP COARSE SALT	1 DL FLOUR
3 L WATER	THE COOKING LIQUID OF THE MEAT, SIEVED (2 L)
1 SMALL ONION	WHITE PEPPER
2 CARROTS	(SALT)
100 G CELERIAC, PEELED	1 DL (ABOUT 50 G)
50 G PARSNIP, PEELED	HORSERADISH, GRATED
2 BAY LEAVES	
1/2 TSP WHOLE WHITE PEPPERS	

BOILED BRISKET OF BEEF WITH HORSERADISH SAUCE

■ Put the brisket, salt and water in a saucepan. Put the saucepan on the hob and carefully remove the foam that appears as the liquid begins to boil. Add the vegetables, cut into large pieces, and the spices, tied into a muslin bag. Simmer on a medium heat for about 2 hours, until the meat is soft. Remove the meat into another dish and strain the stock. Remove the spices and purée the vegetables.

Place a weight on top of the meat and put in a cold place overnight. Cool the stock and remove the fat from its surface. To serve, cut the meat into thin slices and warm it in the oven, moistened with the cooking stock.

■ Begin the preparation of the sauce by melting 50 g butter in a saucepan. Add the flour and mix until smooth. Add the hot stock, mix until smooth, and simmer away one third of the volume. Season the sauce with finely ground white pepper and add salt if necessary. Mix the grated horseradish with the sauce and bring to the boil.

■ Place the sliced brisket and the vegetable purée on plates and serve with the sauce. To drink, a red Côtes du Rhône or an Italian wine from the Veneto region is recommended.

NECK OF PORK
COOKED IN A BEER AND HONEY STOCK

■ Brown the neck of pork pieces in a tablespoonful of butter. Season with salt and pepper and set aside.

Place the rest of the butter in the same pan and fry the sliced onions until brown. Season with the salt, pepper and honey.

Place half the onion and the bay leaf in a lidded oven dish. Place the neck of pork pieces on top of the onion and cover them with onion. Pour the beer into the dish, cover tightly and bake in a 180°C oven for 2–2 1/2 hours.

■ Simmer the potatoes and swedes in separate saucepans until tender. Purée both and mix together with the butter and the boiled cream. Season with salt and nutmeg and, finally, add the chopped parsley.

■ Serve the neck of pork as hot as possible in their juice with the swede-potato purée, and Pilsner-type beer to drink.

4 SERVINGS

	FOR THE SWEDE-POTATO PURÉE:
4 PIECES OF NECK OF PORK	300 G POTATOES, PEELED
OF 170 G, ABOUT 1 1/2 CM	300 G SWEDES, PEELED
THICK	50 G BUTTER
2 TBSP BUTTER	1 DL THIN CREAM
SALT AND FRESHLY GROUND	SALT
WHITE PEPPER	A LITTLE NUTMEG
400 G ONION, PEELED	PARSLEY, CHOPPED
1 – 1 1/2 TBSP RUNNY	
HONEY	
1/2 BAY LEAF	
2 DL DARK BEER	

600 G FILLET OF PORK, CLEANED

300 G SAUERKRAUT

2 DL DRY WHITE WINE

WATER

1 WHOLE CLOVE

1 SMALL ONION

1/2 BAY LEAF

150 G WHITE CABBAGE

150 G SAVOY CABBAGE

SEA SALT

2 TBSP TOMATO PURÉE

1 TBSP BUTTER FOR FRYING

2 TBSP BUTTER FOR BRAISING THE CABBAGE

GENEROUS TSP CORNFLOUR

1 DL SOURED CREAM

1 TBSP SYRUP

SALT AND PEPPER

SADDLE OF PORK WITH THREE CABBAGES

■ Place the sauerkraut in a saucepan. Pour over the white wine and enough water to cover the sauerkraut well. Press the clove into the onion and add it, with the bay leaf, to the sauerkraut. Bring to the boil and simmer, covered, until the sauerkraut is cooked. Pour the sauerkraut into a sieve and reserve the cooking liquid. Remove the onion and the bay leaf.Cut the white cabbage and Savoy cabbage into 1/2 cm strips and simmer until tender in salted water. Cool immediately in cold water to preserve the appearance of the cabbage. Drain well. Cut the pork fillet into 50 g pieces and press them into saddle-shapes.

■ Measure 3 dl of the sauerkraut cooking liquid (supplement with white wine). Stew the tomato purée in 2 tsp butter on a medium heat for 5 minutes. Whisk in the cooking liquid, bring to the boil and thicken with cornflour into which you have mixed a tablespoonful of white wine. Simmer for 5 minutes and whisk in the soured cream and the syrup. Simmer for a few more minutes and season, if necessary, with salt and pepper. Mix the cabbages together with the sauerkraut, season cautiously with salt and pepper, and stew in butter. Keep warm.

■ Season the saddles with salt and pepper and fry them in butter until done. Make a neat pile of the cabbage mixture on each plate, make a pool of the sauce and place the saddles on top. A suitable wine would be a dry, acidic Alsace Riesling.

LAMB MEAT-BALLS
WITH A BROWN BEAN SAUCE

■ Crumble the toast into a bowl and moisten it with the meat stock so that it becomes quite smooth. Add the minced lamb and all the other ingredients and mix to a smooth dough. Place the dough in a cool place for an hour and then form into small balls.

■ Soak the beans for 24 hours in a generous quantity of cold water. Place in a saucepan the soaked beans, the chopped onion and the diced bacon. Pour over the meat stock and wine vinegar and add a little salt, pepper and butter. Heat to boiling point and remove any froth that appears on the surface. Cover the saucepan and simmer gently for 2–2 1/2 hours until the beans are completely tender. Season with syrup so that the sauce acquires a bitter sour-sweet flavour. If necessary, add a little wine vinegar. Mix the cornflour with water and combine with the boiling bean liquid, mixing constantly. The sauce should be a little thickened. Finally, check the seasoning.

■ Fry the meat-balls in butter until done and drain the frying fat. Mix the bean sauce with the meat-balls and serve with fried or puréed potatoes.

   To drink, the best choice is beer or mineral water.

4 SERVINGS

500 G MINCED LAMB

3 PIECES OF TOAST, CRUSTS REMOVED

2 DL COLD MEAT STOCK

2 EGGS

8 COARSELY CRUSHED WHITE PEPPERCORNS

8 COARSELY CRUSHED BLACK PEPPERCORNS

4 COARSELY CRUSHED ALLSPICE PEPPERCORNS

2 TBSP RAW ONION, VERY FINELY CHOPPED

SALT

BUTTER FOR FRYING

FOR THE BROWN BEAN SAUCE:

100 G BROWN KIDNEY BEANS

1 SMALL ONION, CHOPPED

60 G MILD-CURE BACON

3–4 DL MEAT STOCK

3 TBSP RED WINE VINEGAR

SALT, PEPPER

1 TBSP COLD BUTTER

3 TBSP SYRUP

1 TBSP BARLEY- OR CORNFLOUR

3 TBSP WATER

3–4 REINDEER RUMP

(700–800 G)

SALT AND PEPPER

BUTTER FOR FRYING

FOR THE BUCKWHEAT POLENTA:

4 DL WATER

SALT AND PEPPER

120 G HULLED BUCKWHEAT GRAINS

BUTTER

50 G ONION, FINELY CHOPPED

40 G SMOKED REINDEER MEAT, MINCED OR FINELY DICED

2 TBSP PARSLEY, FINELY CHOPPED

8 FINE SLICES OF BACON

FOR THE KOHLRABI GRATIN:

400 G PEELED KOHLRABI

100 G STRONG EMMENTHAL CHEESE

WATER AND SEA SALT

HALF A CLOVE OF GARLIC

BUTTER

2 DL WHIPPING CREAM

1 EGG YOLK

1 EGG

SALT AND PEPPER

GRATED NUTMEG

ROAST REINDEER, WITH BUCKWHEAT POLENTA

■ Boil some salted water, add the buckwheat, stir and simmer on a low heat for 40 minutes to make a thick porridge. Season with salt and pepper. Stew the chopped onion in a little butter and add it to the porridge with the smoked reindeer meat and chopped parsley. Cool until cold. Knead the polenta mixture and form into small balls. Flatten and wrap the bacon slices around them. Cut the kohlrabi and the cheese into 1 cm cubes. Simmer the kohlrabi in salted water until it is almost tender. Plunge it into iced water and drain. Rub a low oven dish with the clove of garlic and butter it. Mix the kohlrabi with the cheese and spread evenly over base of the dish. Mix the cream, the egg yolk and the egg. Season the mixture with salt, pepper and nutmeg and pour into the dish. Bake at 175°C for 35–45 minutes.

■ Let the reindeer steaks rest at room temperature 1 hour. Season them with salt and pepper, brown in a little butter and then place them in a 200°C oven for 12 minutes. Remove the cooked steaks into another dish and keep warm. Fry the buckwheat polenta cakes in butter in a non-stick pan and then put them in a 200°C oven for 10 minutes. Cut the steaks into thin slices, allow two polenta cakes per person and serve the kohlrabi gratin separately. A dark pepper sauce makes a good accompaniment. To drink: a medium full-bodied, softish Gran Reserva Rioja.

BEEF ROLLS WITH A FILLING
OF PICKLED CUCUMBER AND PORK FAT

■ Cut the vegetables into small cubes. Peel the cucumbers, cut off the ends and cut into four lengthwise pieces. Cut the pork fat into eight thin sticks. If the slices of steak are not thin enough, pound them between two sheets of kitchen film. Spread the slices out on a chopping board. With one stick of pork fat and one piece of cucumber per slice, roll them up tightly and secure with a cocktail stick. Heat the oven to 170°C. Heat the butter in a frying pan until it is pale brown in colour. Brown the rolls, add salt and pepper and place them in a casserole. Brown the cubed vegetables in the same pan until they take a little colour and add them to the casserole. Add the bay leaf and half the meat stock. Cover and place in the oven. Bake until the rolls are cooked through, 40–60 minutes depending on the quality of the meat. Place the rolls in another dish and keep warm. Remove the cocktail sticks. Pour the rest of the stock into the casserole and add the anchovy fillet and the mustard. Simmer, covered, until the vegetables are completely tender. Pour the vegetables and the cooking liquid into a liquidiser and purée the sauce until it is as smooth as possible. Add more seasoning if necessary.

■ Pour the sauce over the rolls and bring to the boil. Serve with a potato purée.

A good red wine would be a Corbières or Fitou.

4 SERVINGS

8 HANDSOME, THIN FILLET STEAKS OR

SLICES OF RUMPSTEAK OF 75 G

1 CARROT, PEELED

50 G CELERIAC, PEELED

1 ONION, PEELED

2 RUSSIAN-TYPE PICKLED CUCUMBERS OR

VINEGAR CUCUMBERS

120 G PORK FAT

30 G BUTTER

SALT AND PEPPER

1 BAY LEAF

3 DL MEAT STOCK

1 SMALL ANCHOVY FILLET

1 TSP DIJON MUSTARD

PARSLEY, FINELY CHOPPED

2 THIN STEAKS

50–60 G BEEF MARROW, PREFERABLY IN ONE LARGE PIECE

WATER

COARSELY GROUND SEA SALT

CHIVES

OLIVE OIL

CRUSHED BLACK PEPPERCORNS

2 TBSP GOOD, DARK GRAVY

TWO MINUTE STEAKS
WITH BONE-MARROW FILLING

■ Put the bone marrow in cold water in the refrigerator for 24 hours. Simmer in water seasoned with sea salt until done. Allow to cool a little, then cut into thin slices and return to the cooking liquid.

Chop the chives finely. Brush the minute steaks lightly with olive oil and grill or fry them in a very hot pan, on one side only.

Heat the slices of marrow and place them on the raw side of the steaks. Season with sea salt and coarsely ground pepper and sprinkle generously with chopped chives. Place another steak on top of the first one, raw side up, and place in a 250°C oven for 30 seconds.

■ Spoon a couple of spoonfuls of good, brown gravy around the steak. Serve with, for example, salad. You can also garnish the plate with three or four triangles of sour-dough bread.

This sturdy dish demands a full-bodied red wine, for example from Corbières or Roussillon.

WILLOW GROUSE BREASTS WITH SOURED CREAM SAUCE

■ Remove the breasts from the willow grouse with a sharp knife. Cut the peeled vegetables into 3 cm pieces. Spread the vegetables on the bottom of a wide, buttered oven dish. Chop up the willow grouse carcasses and place them on top of the vegetables. Brown for 20 minutes in a 200°C oven. Add the tomato purée to the oven dish during the browning. Put the browned carcasses and vegetables into a saucepan with the spices. Add the water and cook on a medium heat for 1 hour.

■ Season the breasts with salt and ground white pepper. Melt 1 tbsp butter in the frying pan and brown the breasts on both sides. Remove the breasts into a buttered oven dish and bake in a 200°C oven for 6–7 minutes. Let the meat rest under a cloth for 5 minutes before serving.

■ Add the rest of the butter and the flour to the frying pan. Let the flour brown a little and add 3 dl of the stock from the carcasses. Boil off about one third of the liquid and add the shredded leek and the soured cream. Boil for another 2 minutes.

■ Serve the grouse breasts with the sauce and braised vegetables. To drink, we recommend a light Californian Merlot or a French Côtes de Buzet.

4 SERVINGS

2 WILLOW GROUSE
1 LARGE ONION
150 G CARROTS
200 G CELERY
150 G PARSNIP
2 TBSP TOMATO PURÉE
3 L WATER
3 BAY LEAVES
10 JUNIPER BERRIES, CRUSHED
1 TSP WHOLE WHITE PEPPERCORNS
SALT AND GROUND WHITE PEPPER
2 TBSP BUTTER
1 TBSP FLOUR
50 G GREEN PART OF A LEEK, SHREDDED
1 DL SOURED CREAM

8 SERVINGS

750 G HARE

(ABOUT 6 FILLETS)

2 TBSP COOKING OIL

1 TBSP ROSEMARY,

FINELY CHOPPED

2 TBSP PARSLEY,

FINELY CHOPPED

3 JUNIPER BERRIES, CRUSHED

2 LARGE ONIONS

1 TBSP BUTTER

3 DL COOKED RICE

SALT

GROUND WHITE PEPPER

1 SPRING CABBAGE

2 DL MEAT STOCK

1/2 DL SYRUP

FOR THE SAUCE:

1 TBSP BUTTER

1 TBSP FLOUR

COOKING JUICES

FROM THE HARE

WHIPPING CREAM

SALT, GROUND WHITE PEPPER

ROAST HARE IN CABBAGE LEAVES
IN THE MANNER OF CABBAGE ROLLS

■ Mix the oil with the chopped herbs and the crushed juniper berries. Remove the bones from the hare meat and season it well with the herb mixture. Leave to macerate for a couple of hours. Soften the chopped onions in butter. Add the boiled rice and season the mixture with salt and white pepper.

Remove the stalk and the outer leaves of the cabbage if they are broken. Boil the cabbage in salted water. Remove the leaves as they soften. Let the leaves cool. Thin the central vein of the cabbage leaves with a knife. Place the salted and peppered pieces of hare on the leaves. Spoon the rice–onion mixture over the meat. Fold the cabbage leaves inwards and wrap to make tight parcels. Put the parcels in a buttered oven dish and bake in a 175°C oven for 30–35 minutes. Baste the parcels often during cooking with a mixture of the meat stock and syrup.

■ Melt the butter in a saucepan. Add the flour and cook on a medium heat until the flour browns. Add the cooking juices from the hare and mix until smooth. Add the cream to make a thickish sauce. Finally, season with salt and white pepper.

■ Serve the parcels with the sauce and crushed lingonberries (see page 88).

A red Burgundy from the Côte de Nuits would be a good choice.

WILLOW GROUSE CASSEROLE

■ Remove the bones from the willow grouse. Place the chopped bones in a pan and brown them in butter. Add the cubed carrot, celery and onion and glaze them well. Add water and simmer for about 2 hours. Sieve the stock and continue to simmer until about 2 dl are left. Add the cream and thicken with the butter-flour thickening. Flavour the sauce with the blackcurrant jelly and the blue cheese. Dice the mushrooms and fry them in butter with the finely chopped onions.

■ Melt a little butter in the base of an iron pan. Cut the willow grouse meat into strips and fry them in the butter until they are brown. Pour the gin into the pan and flambé. Season with salt and pepper. Let the sauce come to the boil, but do not simmer it.

■ Serve on to plates straight from the iron pan. Serve wafers made from puff pastry, for example, as an accompaniment.

   A good choice of wine would be a full-bodied Burgundy, for example from the Côte de Beaune area, or a mature Gran Reserva Rioja.

4 SERVINGS

2 WILLOW GROUSE
BUTTER FOR FRYING
1 CARROT
50 G CELERY
2 ONIONS
WATER
2 DL WHIPPING CREAM
1 TBSP BUTTER-FLOUR THICKENING
2 TBSP BLACKCURRANT JELLY
20 G BLUE CHEESE
200 G SHITAKE MUSHROOMS
4 CL GIN
SALT AND PEPPER

DESSERTS

8 DL FROZEN RASPBERRIES, CRANBERRIES, STRAWBERRIES AND

BILBERRIES

200 G CASTER SUGAR

2—3 DL CREAM

ICE-BERRIES
WITH A WARM CARAMEL SAUCE

■ Heat the sugar in a saucepan until it is a handsome brown colour. Add the cream and simmer until the sugar has dissolved completely. Put the icy berries in individual dishes and serve the hot sauce separately.

WARM KAINUU CHEESEBREAD

■ Cut the cheese into portions and place them in an oven-proof roasting dish with sides. Pour the whipping cream into the dish, add the cloudberries and sprinkle the cinnamon-sugar mixture over. Bake for 15 minutes in a 200°C oven.

■ Serve warm, straight from the oven dish.

4 SERVINGS

400 G KAINUU CHEESEBREAD (FINNISH OVEN-FRIED CHEESE)

4 DL CREAM

250 G CLOUDBERRIES

4 TBSP SUGAR

4 TSP CINNAMON

IF ONLY IT WAS CHRISTMAS, SO THAT WE COULD EAT ALL NIGHT!

At the Finnish Christmas table, traditions are still respected. Because Christmas dishes for all the days of Christmas are prepared well in advance, they still consist mainly of foods that can be served cold. Although the Christmas table no longer stands decked from Christmas Eve to the evening of Boxing Day, as was the custom in days gone by, it is part of the tradition for more food to be on offer than it is possible to eat in one sitting. Nevertheless you can be sure that on Christmas night, in addition to Father Christmas's little capped and bearded helpers, much more familiar folk will be illuminated by the pallid light of the refrigerator.

Here are a few classics of the Finnish Christmas table:

1. SALT COD WITH WHITE SAUCE
2. GLASS MASTER'S HERRING
3. FRESH-SALTED SALMON
4. ROES WITH SOURED CREAM AND ONION
5. BRAWN ROLL MADE OF SIDE OF PORK
6. HERRING SALAD OR *ROSOLLI*
7. RICE PUDDING
8. MIXED FRUIT SOUP
9. CHRISTMAS LOAF
10. SWEETENED POTATO CASSEROLE
11. SWEDE CASSEROLE
12. HAM GRATINATED WITH BREADCRUMBS

It is said that Finns begin to celebrate Christmas earlier every year. The reasons are probably as much practical as commercial. Christmas comes at the darkest time of the year and offers a welcome break in the months of cold and darkness. The weeks before Christmas have developed into a kind of substitute for a carnival. Between the first Sunday of advent and Christmas Eve there are far too few days for all the work places, hunting, sauna and sports societies to book venues, food and drink for what is indubitably their most social event of the year. So the celebration of 'little Christmas', which has become almost a folk tradition, often starts in good time in November.

At home, the weeks before Christmas are often celebrated by inviting friends and acquaintances to drink mulled wine. There must be hundreds of recipes for mulled wine, and every hostess and host must have his or her own, the only original version, tried and tested. Here is one more. Let us call it, for the sake of argument, Eero's Excellent.

EERO'S EXCELLENT MULLED WINE

8–10 GLASSES

1 L RED WINE

8 CL KOSKENKORVA VODKA OR

FINNISH EXTRA AQUAVIT

1/2 L BLACKCURRANT WINE

CASTER SUGAR TO TASTE

1 STICK CINNAMON

12 CLOVES

5 CARDEMOM SEEDS

1 LEMON

ALMOND CHIPS AND RAISINS

Mix the red wine, vodka or aquavit with the blackcurrant wine. Add the sugar, spices and grated lemon rind. Mix and set aside overnight. Heat again before serving. Do not allow the liquid to boil, or its most valuable aromas will evaporate into the air. Serve very hot in glasses with almond chips and raisins at their bases.

Finns like to spend their Christmas within the family circle, close to their roots in the peace of the countryside, amid the untouched, snowy landscape.

Finns also believe in Father Christmas and his brownie helpers. And would like others to believe, too – or at least, to know that the only real Father Christmas lives on Korvatunturi mountain, in Finnish Lapland. And for almost all Finns, the Christmases of childhood were white.

From this we can conclude that Christmas and its traditions have a quite special place in Finnish hearts. The same is true, to the greatest possible extent, of traditional Christmas foods. Glass master's herring serves as a good example. For many people, Christmas simply is not Christmas without it.

GLASS MASTER'S HERRING

6 SERVINGS

SALTED ICELANDIC HERRING

WATER, PIECE OF HORSERADISH

2 RED ONIONS, 1 CARROT

1 TSP WHOLE WHITE PEPPERS

1 TSP MUSTARD SEEDS

PIECE OF GINGER, 2 BAY LEAVES

FOR THE VINEGAR SAUCE

3 DL PRESERVING VINEGAR

1 DL SUGAR

Clean the herring; leave the skin, but remove all the scales and fins. Soak in water for 8 hours. Drain the herring and cut it into 2–3 cm slices. Cut the horseradish into cubes. Slice the peeled onion and carrots. Pile the herring, vegetables and spices in layers into a glass jar. Bring the sauce to the boil, cool it and pour over the herring. Keep in a cool place for 2–3 days.

Ham is the king of the Christmas table. Its supremacy will not be challenged by turkey or goose, which have become much more common in recent years, for a long time. In the matter of the salting and preparation of ham, there is no shortage of recipes. Most people now buy their ham ready salted and roast it in a medium oven. Roasted gently for hours, the ham becomes succulent throughout. We salted our own ham and cooked it in the traditional manner: boiling. We removed the skin from the cooked ham and gratinated the surface with a mixture of mustard and breadcrumbs bound with egg yolk. Ten minutes in a hot oven gives the ham a fine, golden-brown surface. Finally, we garnished the surface with whole cloves. Peas and prunes and vegetable casseroles are the natural accompaniments of ham. Swede casserole and sweetened potato casserole originated as part of the ancient Finnish tradition of everyday food. Carrot and liver casseroles, for their part, represent a typically western Finnish gastronomic tradition.

Mixed fruit soup and prune pudding are no longer common desserts of the Christmas table, but they are a reminder of the times when the exotic fruits of the south arrived on the shop shelves dried, once a year, conveniently just before Christmas.

Salt cod, like glass master's herring, found its way to the Finnish Christmas table via the Swedish gentry. It is a dish that still divides the nation in two more comprehensively than any linguistic or cultural wall. For some of the friends of salt cod, it is the fish itself that is best, while others are equally convinced that the secret of the dish lies in the white sauce that is served with the fish.

MIXED FRUIT SOUP

6 SERVINGS

150 G DRIED MIXED FRUIT

1 L WATER, 1 DL SUGAR

1 STICK CINNAMON

1 TBSP POTATO FLOUR

1 TBSP LEMON JUICE

Rinse the mixed fruit in cold water. Measure the water and sugar into a saucepan. Soak the fruit in the sugared water overnight. Add the cinnamon stick. Boil on a medium heat for half an hour. Remove the cinnamon stick and lift the fruit carefully into a serving bowl. Mix the potato flour with a little cold water. Heat the syrup until it boils and mix in the potato flour mixture. Do not allow the syrup to boil again. Pour the syrup into the serving dish over the fruit. Serve cold with whipped cream.

Weight, Measures, and Temperatures

WEIGHTS

1 pound (lb.) = 16 ounces = 453.6 grams (g)
1 ounce (oz.) = 28.35 g
1 kilogram (kg) = 1000 g = 2 lbs 3 oz.
100 g = 3.5 oz.

MEASURES

1 US gallon = 4 liquid quarts = 3.785 litres (l)
1 liquid quart = 2 liquid pints = 9.5 decilitres (dl)
1 liquid pint = 16 US fl. oz. = 4.73 dl
1 cup = 8 US oz. = 29.6 millilitres (ml)
1 quart (dry) = 1.1 litres
1 litre = 10 dl = (more than) 2 pints
1 decilitre = (less than) 1/2 cup

TEMPERATURES

Fahrenheit	Centigrade
268 °F	131 °C
350 °F	177 °C
375–400 °F	190–204 °C
450–500 °F	232–260 °C

Centigrade	Fahrenheit
100 °C	212 °F
200 °C	392 °F
250 °C	382 °F
300 °C	572 °F